SCENE
AND
STRUCTURE

ABOUT THE AUTHOR

Jack M. Bickham is the author of more than 80 published novels, some of which have been made into films. He has also written several other instructional books, including *Writing Novels That Sell* and *The 38 Most Common Fiction Writing Mistakes (and How to Avoid Them)*. The themes of scene and structure are an important element of Bickham's fiction instruction, whether in books, magazine articles or lectures.

SCENE
AND
STRUCTURE

BY

JACK M. BICKHAM

CINCINNATI, OHIO

Scene and Structure. Copyright © 1993 by Jack M. Bickham. Printed and bound in the United States of America. All rights reserved. No part of this book may be reproduced in any form or by any electronic or mechanical means including information storage and retrieval systems without permission in writing from the publisher, except by a reviewer, who may quote brief passages in a review. Published by Writer's Digest Books, an imprint of F&W Publications, Inc., 1507 Dana Avenue, Cincinnati, Ohio 45207; 1-800-289-0963. First edition.

This hardcover edition of *Scene and Structure* features a "self-jacket" that eliminates the need for a separate dust jacket. It provides sturdy protection for your book while it saves paper, trees and energy.

97 96 95 94 93   5 4 3 2 1

Library of Congress Cataloging-in-Publication Data

Bickham, Jack M.
    Scene and structure / by Jack M. Bickham.
        p.   cm.
    Includes index.
    ISBN 0-89879-551-6
    1. Fiction—Technique.   I. Title.
PN3365.B49   1993
808.3—dc20   92-32134
                                        CIP

Edited by Jack Heffron

This book is dedicated to the memory of Dwight V. Swain: writer, teacher and friend. Without him, I would have had no career as a novelist.

—J.M.B.

CONTENTS

CHAPTER 1

THE STRUCTURE OF MODERN FICTION

MENTION WORDS SUCH AS STRUCTURE, form, or plot to some fiction writers, and they blanch. Such folks tend to believe that this kind of terminology means writing by some type of formula or predetermined format as rigid as a paint-by-numbers portrait.

Nothing could be further from the truth.

In reality, a thorough understanding and use of fiction's classic structural patterns *frees* the writer from having to worry about the wrong things, and allows her to concentrate her imagination on characters and events rather than on such stuff as transitions and moving characters around, when to begin or open a chapter, whether there ought to be a flashback, and so on. Once you understand structure, many such architectural questions become virtually irrelevant—and structure has nothing to do with "filling in the blocks."

Structure is nothing more than a way of looking at your story material so that it's organized in a way that's both logical and dramatic. Structure is a process, not a rigid format. Structure in fiction is not static, but dynamic.

We need structure in our fiction for many reasons, but the main one goes to understanding. We need structure (a) as writers, so our stories will "hold together" and make sense. We need structure (b) as readers, so we can understand this story we're reading, and *feel* something as a result.

The structure of a story is internal. It's a bit different from form. The form of a story is external. The two interrelate, but they're not exactly the same thing. Structure is more like the pattern of 2×4s, braces and other materials inside your house. Form has to do with *what's been done with the structure*—whether the house is colonial or contemporary, large or small, one- or two-story, for example.

Obviously, however, it's hard to talk about structure without considering form, and *vice versa*. A builder planning to build in the *form* of a ten-floor office building would not use all the same construction materials in the walls—or other *structural* components—that he would in building a one-floor bungalow. On the other hand (lucky for the builder!) many of the same principles of construction would apply to both projects. In both he would have to remember that there are practical limits to how long a span can be without bracing of some kind, for example—and in both he might want to remember that a building needs a solid foundation and a good roof! Thus, whatever his form, his fundamental principles of structure would be the same.

It's the same in fiction. Story length, author intention, traditional expectations of the audience, and all sorts of things may affect the form a story may take. But underneath most forms lies the same structure—the same unchanging principles, the same creative laws.

Those are what this book is mainly about.

The short story writer is taught that a short story has "a beginning, a middle and an end," or perhaps "a situation, a complication, a climax and a denouement." The novelist may hear advice such as "paint a broader picture," or "give the characters more depth," or even "make all your chapters twenty pages long"—none of it very darned helpful when you're sitting at your word processor with tiny droplets of blood oozing from your forehead. But once you understand structure, you'll see with growing clarity that short story and novel alike have many of the same basic elements of *structure*—so that whatever your *form*, long or short or in the middle, you can always work with the same basics.

THE HISTORY OF STRUCTURE

This wasn't always true. The first English novelists, for example, knew they wanted a very-long-story form. They had epic poems as their only obvious guideline. Literary historians generally agree, however, that the first novels in the English language had a far simpler form and internal structure than much earlier long narrative poems such as *Beowulf*.

In writing for a broad, popular audience (they hoped!), the first neo-novelists came up with a very simple device: the personal letter. The letter itself had no formal internal structure beyond that of [salutation]+[reporting and comment]+[signature]. A sequential series of such relatively unstructured letters became the form for the book.

The earliest English novelists like Richardson used this device well. The letter, however, always removed the reader somewhat from the action because everything had to be told—obviously—some time after the event actually took place.

Writers who took the next step in developing internal structure for the long prose narrative made it a small step: They built their novels around a series of entries in a journal or diary (*Robinson Crusoe* being a good example). This form allowed a bit more informal personal commentary on the action by the writer, and also worked well at the time. Again, however, the reader was being *told* the story after it took place, rather than seeming to experience it as it unfolded. And even a journal or diary was obviously a literary device that took a certain amount of extra imaginative effort on the part of the reader if he was to "really get into it."

The next step, also a short one, was more significant because it tried to attack the limitation problems of letter-diary-journal structure. This was the adoption of a "conversational" structure with the first-person narrator writing you, the reader, his story as if he were telling it to you in his living room, with all the asides, explanations to "dear reader" and loose associational tone that such a structure allowed. More important, in jettisoning the "documentary" approach, it freed the novelist to tell the story more as if it were happening in the story "now" rather than as something being documented after the event; in other words, it added some sense of immediacy.

It was only after all these early experiments had been tried that later novelists—notably the greatest of them all, Charles Dickens—began developing the kind of structure more familiar to modern readers: a sequence of *scenes* played in the story here-and-now as if they were taking place as the reader read and imagined them, and told (often first person) from the viewpoint of a character in the series of scenes as they took place.

Novels and short stories structured around letters, diaries or author conversation use time-honored devices, and you can find an occasional novel of one or another of these types that achieves success. There are, however, a number of other general forms.

TYPES OF FORMS

The first-person novel, told by a character inside the story action, remains a form that is often seen today. It offers the strength of seeming actuality, and helps the reader identify with the central character because only the story "I" ever shares thoughts or feelings.

More common today is the story told in the third person, but with the viewpoint limited to only one character within the story action. This is almost always the character with the most to win or lose as the story unfolds—a hero or heroine.

More ambitious (in terms of length) novels often slightly alter this form, still telling the story in the third person, but jumping around to many character viewpoints. It is a measure of the sophistication of the novel today, however, that careful study will usually show that the viewpoint in such multiple-viewpoint novels remains limited to a single character in most structural compartments or scenes of the book.

And of course there are other, less-common forms of the novel today such as stream of consciousness, wherein the reader is plunged into the almost-chaotic ruminations of a character's wandering mind; the "document novel," in which medical records or the contents of a computer data bank or some such are presented in seemingly chaotic form to tell someone's story indirectly through the documentation; and what might be called the "collection novel," in which a series of short stories is presented between one set of covers and the reader is left to find their common denominator—or not—as she can.

The point to be made here, however, is that at least 95 percent of the popular novels published today—whatever their general form—depend on the structure of the *scene* to make them work.

To put this a slightly different way: Most successful fiction today is based on a structure that uses a series of *scenes* that interconnect in a very clear way to form a long narrative with linear development from the posing of a story question at the outset to the answering of that question at the climax.

In the chapters to follow, we'll look at some general fiction strategy, then examine the internal structure of the scene—and how a series of scenes can be linked into a larger architectural plan to form the modern story. We'll concentrate on the novel form, because such a long form makes scene structure most necessary as a way of maintaining logic and pace. But whether your form is short or long, you'll find that an ability to plan, write, and then link scenes is the key to effective storytelling in today's world.

CHAPTER 2

STRATEGY: HOW TO START YOUR STORY AND HOW TO END IT

IN CHAPTER 1 YOU GOT a glimpse of how structure relates to form, and how the internal structure of the modern novel developed out of simpler forms. Before getting down to the nuts and bolts of the new structure, however, we'd better take a general look at how popular narrative fiction works—or ought to.

In doing so, we'll not only get a clearer picture of the general form and strategy of long fiction today, but we'll also hope to give some insight into some of the questions that always seem to plague novice novelists. Questions such as—

- "How long should my novel be?"
- "Where should I start my story?"
- "How and when should I end my story?"
- "Do I need a lot of subplots?"
- "Does it have to have a happy ending?"

And so on!

The answer to the first common question—about length—may be answered in a general way: Length may be determined by the requirements of your publisher, especially if you plan to work in a genre. Harlequin romances, for example, are written to a rigid length requirement. On the other hand, if you have no such genre or publisher guidance, then you should plan to keep your novel's length somewhere between 60,000 and 90,000 words.

(You may be wondering how many manuscript pages these totals represent. The answer is not clear-cut, since the typeface size you use on your typewriter or printer will determine the average number of words per page. Also, a story with a considerable amount of brief dialogue—many partial lines per page—may average considerably fewer words per page than a manuscript with little dialogue and a great amount of long-paragraph narration or description. As a general rule of thumb, start out with the assumption that the 60,000- to 90,000-word parameters represent page-lengths in the range of 240 to 360 finished pages. But to be sure about your own averages, the best advice is to count — carefully — the number of words on ten filled pages pulled at random from your manuscript; then determine your own average.)

Books shorter than 60,000 words are published, certainly, and a novel of 50,000 words has a chance. But lengths falling far below the 60,000-word norm are rarities that many publishers don't often buy because they don't fit traditional production and selling strategies. Books longer than 90,000 words are very expensive to publish, will cost more at the bookstore, and consequently represent what may be an unacceptable risk for many publishers.

Granted, this still leaves an area for potential confusion about *your* manuscript and how long it should be. But once you have a general idea of story strategy, your worries about length and many other problems will be eased. So let's look.

YOU ARE HERE

There was a wonderful time, not so long ago, when a writer planning to produce a novel could start virtually with her main character's birth, or at least as early as his early childhood, and simply tell almost the entire story of a person's life. But readers today are more hurried and impatient — and jaded by swiftly paced television drama; they want condensation, speed and punch.

(This was nowhere more vividly demonstrated to me than in a recent conversation with a high school senior. He was moaning about having to read *A Tale of Two Cities*. Asked why he was experiencing difficulty with the book, he said, "It's boring!" So, if readers today can think *A Tale of Two Cities* is boring, we'd all better learn the fastest-moving, tightest methods of telling a story that we can discover.)

So it's not very likely that you're going to be able to start page 1 of your story "at the beginning" *as you may have imagined it* in planning the entire flow of the yarn. You are going to have to find a time later than a character's birth or earliest childhood.

Similarly, it's not very likely that you're going to find any readers patient enough to wade through practically every interesting event in your character's life, all the way to his death, even if you start your story well into that life. You've got to select!

How, then, do you know where to start?

Generally, as implied in chapter 1, most storytellers today, even novelists, try to start their story as late in the total imagined chronology of events as is possible. Given the imagined sixty-year lifetime of a main character, the professional writer today will pinpoint those few days, weeks or months in the character's life span that form the dramatic core of his existence; the writer will then present only that brief time span in the manuscript — starting on June 10 of the character's forty-fourth year, for example, ending on July 4 of the same year, perhaps flashing back to earlier life events (but only if *absolutely* necessary), and giving nothing whatsoever of later events in the character's long life.

It will help you to select such a late starting point and early ending point for your story if you will remember the following facts about readers:

1. They are fascinated and threatened by significant change;
2. They want the story to start with such a change;
3. They want to have a story question to worry about;
4. They want the story question answered in the story ending;
5. They will quickly lose patience with everything but material that relates to the story question.

What follows is an explanation of these points.

Readers are fascinated and threatened by change in their real lives, and nothing else fascinates or threatens them so much in fiction. Why?

Because each of us carries around inside ourselves a mental picture of the kind of person we are. "I'm an efficient secretary," we may say. Or, "I'm an outdoorsman who loves to hunt." Or, "I'm a hometown boy not interested in travel far from home." This *self-concept* is at the heart of our opinion of ourselves—how much we like ourselves, how much confidence we feel, etc.—and we live our lives in large measure to be in consonance with this self-concept, and to enhance it. Our self-concept is our most precious mental and emotional possession.

Any significant *change* can and probably will threaten the self-concept. Suppose the woman who defines herself as an efficient secretary is suddenly confronted by a new office situation so chaotic (or filled with new and confusing computer equipment, let us say) that she no longer can feel that she is operating at peak efficiency. In other words, some external change in her environment (the office situation) has put her out of kilter *vis-à-vis* her self-concept. In such a case, the woman who defines herself as an efficient secretary is going to be worse than unhappy; she is going to be profoundly shaken. If she is to be happy again, she will have to take some action. She may struggle to learn about computer systems to regain her old efficiency; she may quit her job and find a simpler one; she may try to convince the boss to go back to the old way of doing things in the office; she may elect some other course of action that will somehow get her self-concept back in tune with her everyday reality.

You may be thinking that the simplest thing for our secretary to do would be change her self-concept to something like, "I'm an old-fashioned kind of office worker who doesn't learn new tricks." But it's been psychologically proven that the self-concept is so deeply engrained, and so devoutly protected, that most people will go to almost any lengths to protect it *as it stands today.*

If you wish to see this concept in action, you may consider any number of classic or popular novels, such as Dickens's *Great Expectations*, in which Pip's life is profoundly changed at the outset and he is off to London; *The Dreadful Lemon Sky*, one of the Travis McGee novels by John D. Mac-

Donald, which begins with the shattering sound of McGee's burglar alarm being tripped by an unexpected, desperate visitor; John Steinbeck's *The Winter of Our Discontent*, opening with an inheritance and a banker's challenge to make a risky investment; *Prelude to Terror*, by Helen MacInnes, in which a man leaves his lodgings and is followed by a sinister character; *Forfeit*, by Dick Francis, in which a man dies and a letter arrives—all in the first sentence; the classic opening of *The Savage Day*, by Jack Higgins, in which an imprisoned man has an unexpected caller and as the narrator says bluntly, "everything changed" (see Appendix 1, Excerpt 1), or even my own novel, *Twister*, which begins with a tornado. Once aware of the principle, you will notice examples all around you in the stories you read.

What does this say to you as a writer? Simply this:

For maximum effectiveness, you should start your story at the time of the change that threatens your major character's self-concept.

You will determine what this change will be in your story by thinking about your main character in considerable depth. Having done so, you will then write down his self-concept in a maximum of ten or fifteen words. You will then devise a fictional event that will represent threatening change to him, make him feel miserable and out of sync with his environment—and ready to struggle to make himself "feel right" again.

To put all this another way: Significant change that threatens your character's self-concept is where your story starts.

It may be a birth, a death, a wedding, a divorce, a telephone call, a letter, a visit by an old friend, a new family moving in down the block, or the turning of the first leaf of autumn. If it's a change, and if it threatens the character, then it's a good place to start chapter 1.

Knowing this, you can much more easily decide where your own tale is to begin on paper. No matter how wonderfully interesting those first thirty years of your character's life may have been, you can probably jettison almost all of them if the change that *this* story is about happens when he is age thirty-one. In like fashion, you may have imagined that said character will live until age sixty or beyond. But you don't have to tell about all the later years of his life, either, because *this* story stops when he has gotten himself straightened around again in terms of his self-concept as it relates to *this* change that you started with on page 1.

Now consider your reader's psychological reactions when confronted with a concept-threatening change in the opening of your novel. Mr. Reader begins to worry. So far, so good; he may be willing to worry for a long time. But in today's hurried, impatient world, that Reader can't be expected to worry passively about the same vague and unchanging bad situation for several hundred pages. He needs something a bit more concrete to worry about.

You meet that need at the outset of your story when you show your character coming up with a vital *intention* or *story goal*, designed to "fix things" for him in terms of his sensation of being out of equilibrium with his environment. Every good fiction character is thus goal-motivated.

The moment your character thinks or says aloud what his goal is— as a result of the change and the need to fix things—you can count on your reader to latch onto that stated goal like a lifeline. The moment your character states his *goal*, the reader will begin to worry about that — will follow every later story incident and interpret its meaning in terms of your character's struggle toward that goal — will turn the goal statement into a *story question* — and keep reading avidly as long as the action relates to the question.

So a story starts with change, which leads to a goal, which raises a story question in the reader's mind.

But how do you end the novel? You do so by *answering the story question you posed at the outset.*

Thus, if your story began with the secretary shocked and scared because of the change in her office environment, your next step had to be the selection of her intention designed to fix things. Let's say you decided that *she* decided to learn how to operate the new computer system, or bust. The reader at this point can be trusted to translate this goal into a story question, and begin reading to learn the answer to "*Will* she learn the new computer system?" When you answer that question, the story ends.

This answering, which takes place at the climax of your story, must answer the question you asked. You can't cheat here. You can't end with a climax that shows her accepting a marriage proposal, for example, or falling down a flight of stairs, or winning the Florida lottery. Your reader has worried about "*Will* she learn the new computer system?" and that's what you have to answer; nothing other or less will do!

Do you see now how the sketchiest understanding of self-concept and the threat of change will help you decide where your novel starts, and where it ends? I hope so. This understanding helps answer several of our nagging questions:

How long should your story be? As long as it takes (within the general physical page limits mentioned earlier) to answer the story question you pose at the outset.

Where should you start? At the moment of threatening change.

How and when should you end the story? By answering the story question, however you have to show this to your reader and whenever in story time the answer is found.

Do you need a lot of subplots? No. But you can certainly have some *if they are relevant to the story question.*

And does it have to be a happy ending? By no means. It has to be a *fitting* ending — an ending that answers the story question.

A GAME PLAN

So how are you to use this information in the most practical way? Here is a brief "game plan" you might try:

1. Consider your story materials as presently imagined. Look for and identify, in terms of days, weeks or months, that briefer period of time

when "the big stuff happens." Plan to eliminate virtually everything else.

2. Think hard about your most major character and what makes him tick—what his self-concept is, and what kind of life he has built to protect and enhance it. (Make sure that this character is the type who will struggle if threatened. Wimps won't form a story goal or strive toward it.)

3. Identify or create a dramatic situation or event which will present your character (and your reader) with the significant, threatening moment of change.

4. Plan your plot so that your novel will open with this event.

5. Decide what intention or goal your most significant character will select to try to fix things after the threatening opening change. Note what story question this goal will put in the reader's mind.

6. Devise the start of a plan formulated by your most significant character as he sets out to make things right again.

7. Figure out how much later—and where and how—the story question finally will be answered. You should strive to know this resolution before you start writing. Granted, the precise time and even the place and details of the outcome may be changed by how your story works out in the first draft. But—even recognizing that your plan for the resolution may change later—you should have more than a vague idea when you begin. (To use a somewhat farfetched example, a ship captain might begin a voyage planning to unload his cargo in faraway England; war or weather *en route* might finally dictate that he would unload in France; but if he had set sail with no idea of his cargo and no idea of an intended destination or route, he might have wound up in Africa . . . or the North Sea . . . or sailing aimlessly and endlessly until he ran out of fuel—or sank. A novelist, like a ship captain, should have a good idea of where he plans to end up.)

8. Plan to make the start and end as close together in time as you can, and still have room for a minimum of 50,000 words of dramatic development.

Having made these key decisions, you will have gone far toward answering all those common nagging questions listed at the start of this chapter. And you'll also be well on your way to understanding the functional form of the modern story.

As an example of how all this works, let me mention one of my own novels, *Miracleworker*. In this medical thriller, a country doctor has been using experimental drugs on patients—often with disastrous results—for more than a decade. The female physician who is the central figure in the novel grew up admiring the now-old man, and has known him for more than thirty years, but is unaware of his misdeeds. In the story, she is to return to the old hometown, slowly learn the old doctor's terrible secret, and reveal it to the world after a personal crisis and great physical danger.

In selecting a time for the novel to start (as late in the action as possible), I chose a letter from the old doctor inviting her to come visit for a part of the summer and help him at his clinic. As an ending, I chose to have my heroine almost killed by an accomplice intent on hiding the doctor's secret only about five weeks after her arrival. The opening letter constituted a *change*, which threatened my heroine because she feared her old idol might be dying; proud of her own skills and intensely loyal to the old doctor (major components of her *self-concept*), she goes with the *goal* of helping him regain his health, but an unexpected patient death arouses her reluctant suspicions, setting her onto a *plan of action* to find out what has really been happening in the town, with the *resolution* forced quickly when a doctor's associate decides the heroine must be killed to keep things secret.

Much later in this book we'll look considerably deeper into story development. But before that discussion can make much sense to you, we have to examine some of the basic structural building blocks—the pieces you fit together to get from A to Z—from the opening threat of change to the answering of the story question.

We start doing that in the next chapter.

See Appendix 1.

CHAPTER 3

STRUCTURE IN MICROCOSM: CAUSE AND EFFECT

WHEN MOST NONWRITERS TALK ABOUT "form" or "structure," they reverse the usual cliché and can't see the trees for the forest. They look at book-length elements—or even such nonstructural aspects as theme—and seldom get down to the nitty-gritty where modern fiction structure really begins. As a writer, however, you can't afford to do that. You need to understand structure in the larger elements (which will come later), but first you need to understand how the same structural principles work almost line-by-line in the modern story.

We're talking here about the simple laws of cause and effect, stimulus and response. Until you understand these perfectly, and can apply them in your fiction with unerring expertise, you can't hope to understand anything bigger in terms of structure.

CAUSE AND EFFECT

So what do cause and effect, stimulus and response, have to do with the structure of fiction?

Everything, that's all.

In the real, everyday world, accident, coincidence and fate often play a major role in determining "how things work out" in a person's life. Bad things happen to good people for no reason, and as today's politics all too often proves, the opposite is equally true. Given such evident random meaninglessness in real life, people sometimes grow cynical, or join the bad guys, or give up. Things often don't make much sense.

In most popular fiction, the situation is quite different. While the workings of luck, coincidence, fate, etc., may be shown from time to time, *fiction must make more sense than real life* if general readers are to find it credible. So, for example, in real life someone may fall ill for no apparent reason and with no evident cause. In fiction, the character would have to be seen depressed about recent developments and tired from overwork; he would then have to be seen walking into an office or home where people were already sick with the dread illness; and then one of the sick persons might even have to sneeze in his face—all before the reader would find credible what in real life would happen without apparent cause.

To restate this differently: in fiction, *effects* (plot developments) must have *causes* (background), and vice versa. If you want someone to fall ill (and want the reader to believe it!), you must first build in the background (perhaps a raging epidemic), a character who is overworked and weary, and who also is depressed enough to have a poorly functioning immune system, and then you have to provide the more immediate (present story time) cause, the entering of the house and finally the deadly sneeze.

Much of plotting from chapter to chapter deals with this kind of juggling of events so that one thing leads logically to another, cause-and-effect fashion. Writers over the years have probably sweated enough to fill Lake Erie as they tried to figure out *how* to motivate Priscilla to open the locked door (cause), or *what next* might happen after she did so (effect).

In real life, blind luck has to be accepted because, after all, there it is—it just happened, period. But the fiction reader demands more credibility than he usually gets in real life. So it's up to you, the fiction writer, to build your story in such a way that every cause you put in has an effect downstream in the story, sooner or later (and preferably sooner!), and for every effect you plot out, you have to figure out a cause that would make it happen.

Once you are good at this as a writer, you can make almost anything happen in your story; all you have to do is figure out what is to cause it. And once you have had *that* particular thing happen with good reason, then your next plotting step is infinitely simpler because all you have to do is take the next logical step and ask yourself, "Now that that has happened, what does it, in turn, cause to happen?"

However, this kind of cause-and-effect planning and story presentation does more than simply help the reader suspend disbelief. Because this kind of presentation shows a world in which things *do* make sense—in which everything isn't just meaningless chaos and chance—the resulting story also has the effect of offering a little hope to the reader: a suggestion by implication that life doesn't have to be meaningless, and that bad things don't always have to happen to good people for no reason . . . a hint that maybe the reader can seize some control of his own life after all, and that good effort may sometimes actually pay off—and our existence may indeed even have some kind of meaning.

For a person like me, who isn't blessed with a very deep mind, the more far-reaching implications of this type of cause-and-effect rationality in fiction seem to be very far-reaching and important indeed. I suspect that when you write a story that makes sense through use of cause and effect, you are also implying, somehow, that life is worth living. Personally I like that.

So if you think at all as I do—or even if you don't, but would like to produce fiction that makes sense and has appeal—I hope you will ponder often and deeply about causes and effects in your own fiction. Look at every turn in the story—every event—and make sure that there is cause for it. Look for causes on which you may not have followed up with resulting events. For to do otherwise is to invite disbelief (at best) on the part of your readership.

I remember, for example, a student story handed in to me once at the University of Oklahoma. In this particular story, there was a violent windstorm at night, to which much description was devoted. (This made it a big cause of something, right?) But in the morning, none of the story characters mentioned it, the sun was shining, and the lawns beyond the house windows did not have so much as a blown-down leaf on them. It was easy enough to fix, but the writer had forgotten entirely to show the *effect* of the storm; if she had sent the story out in its present condition, it would have lost credibility for the editor-reader at that point very early in the going because a strong *cause* had been shown and its *effects* had to be shown as well, even if briefly—leaves on the lawns, perhaps a broken tree limb, comments by a character or two about the aftermath. All this could have been done very briefly, but it *had to be done*.

Similarly, I recall another student's novel in which the hero and the villain were together in a small starship hurtling through space. Suddenly the engines went dead and the two archenemies saw that they had only one escape pod—meaning one would live and one would die. This was all fine, but the story lost credibility for me at the instant the engines failed. Why? Because it was just *bad luck*. An effect had been presented without cause. (Again, it was easy enough to fix: The writer put in a brief segment ahead of the engine failure, showing the villain sabotaging it. Of course *that* required a bit of villain-motivation, showing why the villain thought it was a good idea, but again this could have been handled quite briefly by showing the villain intending only to slow the engines so his cronies might catch up, or some such.)

Please note that most such cause-effect story repairs can be handled in a few words. The key point here is not to exhaust the reader with great details, but simply to make sure that author-inserted causes are shown to have effects, and author-desired effects can be seen to have had causes.

STIMULUS AND RESPONSE

Cause and effect, however, are not operative only in such larger fiction elements as background, character motive, etc. Cause and effect work at an even more minute level, where they surface in the form of physical *stimulus and response*—and are every bit as important.

Stimulus and response are cause and effect made more specific and immediate. They function right now in the story, this instant—this punch making the other man duck, for example, or this question making the other person reply at once, or this bolt of lightning making Sally jump out of her shoes in fright.

Again, in real life we may see people do things for no apparent immediate reason. We may witness responses for which we can't find stimulus. A man or woman may burst into tears in the midst of what seems to us a perfectly casual conversation. Or Sally may jump in sudden fright for some reason we can't see or hear at all.

Conversely, we may—in real life—see stimuli for which we would expect an immediate response, and yet get—nothing. Joe may say, "I feel terribly depressed" (a strong stimulus), yet his friend Mary may reply as if no verbal stimulus was sent, saying nothing at all or maybe saying something like, "It was certainly an exciting game Saturday." You may stop a stranger on the street to ask directions, and receive no response whatsoever, not even a silent, hostile stare.

Such responses without stimuli or stimuli that get no discernible response are believable in everyday life, of course, because—as in the case of larger cause-and-effect elements—the incredible transaction is simply *there*, in the actual world, and one can hardly refuse to believe the evidence before one's own eyes.

We constantly struggle to make our fiction credible, however, because our readers can at any moment stop believing our story. Therefore, in even the simplest transactions in fiction, we must always remember a few simple rules:

- Stimulus must be external—that is, action or dialogue, something that could be witnessed if the transaction were on a stage.
- Response must also be external in the same way.
- For every stimulus, you must show a response.
- For every desired response, you must provide a stimulus.
- Response usually must follow stimulus *at once*.
- When response to stimulus is not logical on the surface, you must ordinarily explain it.

A few examples should make these rules clearer in your mind.

Let's suppose you have a segment in your story where Joe and Sam are playing catch with a baseball in the front yard. If you show the following stimulus—

Joe threw the ball to Sam.

Then you must show Sam's response, such as—

Sam caught it. (*or*)
Sam dropped it. (*or*)
Sam didn't see it and it hit him in the nose.

Or something of a similar, immediate response-nature.

How can something as simple as this get messed up? One sees it messed up all the time. Consider this transaction:

(*Stimulus*) Joe threw the ball to Sam.
"Sure is a nice day!" Sam said.

Now, some might think this is fine, because the reader will assume that Sam caught the ball. I'm afraid that many, many readers, however, will *not* make that assumption, and a tiny tickle of disbelief will begin far back in their brain somewhere—the obvious question: *What happened to the ball???*

How do you fix such slips? By showing the completion of the stimulus-response transaction, by providing the response to the stimulus you've already shown, thus:

> (*Stimulus*) Joe threw the ball to Sam.
> (*Response*) Sam caught it. "Sure is a nice day to play catch!"

Now this very simple transaction makes sense because the response to Joe's specific stimulus has been shown. But if you are writing a bit of action like this, please note that you have to stay alert! After Sam caught the ball, completing that stimulus-response transaction, what did he do? He started another one. He *said something*. So what has to happen next? Of course: *Joe has to answer him.*

Another example, this time of a response without evident stimulus, might be the following:

> Mary walked into the party.
> "Oh, no!" Julie groaned, and ran for the exit.

What's wrong here? Well, evidently Mary's walking into the party must somehow be intended as a stimulus for Julie's groan and fast exit. But if we want Julie to show a response of groaning and running, we have to give her a better, clearer reason for so doing—a better stimulus.

Again, the matter might be easily fixed in several ways. Here is an obvious one:

> Mary walked into the party, wearing a strapless blue gown.
> "Oh no!" Julie—wearing an identical dress—groaned, and ran for
> the exit.

Of such simple "fixes" is credible fiction made.

Of course it might have been possible, in terms of the above transaction, to build in a bit of *background* prior to the incident—perhaps showing Julie's purchase of her blue strapless gown, the importance of the party to her, and her lurking terror of looking anything like archrival Mary at such a big event. If the writer had given this background shortly before the stimulus-response transaction, then it *might* have been okay as first written. The points to be amplified here, however, remain constant: If something is to be a stimulus, it must *clearly* be a stimulus, and it must happen right now. If something is to be a response, it must *clearly* be a response to the stimulus immediately preceding it, and it must happen right now.

The "right now" phraseology is not incidental. You can imagine, I'm sure, how incredible it would be for a reader if the writer showed some strong stimulus, and then it took the other character hours or days to react. Something like:

> (*Stimulus*) "I'm sorry, Frank. Your mother just died."
> (*Response*) Six hours later, Frank fainted with shock.

A perfectly believable response, if it hadn't taken all that time to come.

To put all this another way, you can mess up stimulus-response transactions three ways:

1. You can show a stimulus and then show no external response (or perhaps one that doesn't fit or doesn't make sense);
2. You can show a character response when no stimulus (or no credible one) for it has been shown; or
3. You can put so much story time between stimulus and response that the logical relationship between the two events is no longer evident.

But what, you may ask, about those stimulus-response transactions which would make perfectly good sense *if we just knew what the receiving character thought and felt* before responding? In such cases, where the stimulus-response transaction is complicated, we must keep things clear for the reader by showing him the character's *internalization* — the feeling-thought process that goes between the stimulus and the response.

If you stop to think about it, even the most obvious stimulus-response transaction requires some internal messaging in the mind and body of the receiver of the stimulus. Even if you touch something hot and jerk back instantly, what really happened was that a message went up your arm to some part of your brain — *"Pain down here!"* — and your brain sent a reflexive message back down the arm again — *"Jerk away from it!"*

Such simple transactions, of course, don't need an explanation, any more than did Joe's throwing the ball and Sam's catching it. But the internalization process always takes place, and when things are complicated, you may need to remember that the pattern of every stimulus-response transaction — in deepest reality — is:

STIMULUS — INTERNALIZATION — RESPONSE

The rule being that you present the internalization to the reader — "play" it for him, if you will — when necessary to make an otherwise superficially incredible transaction understandable and credible.

One or two examples should show how this works.

Suppose you have the following in your manuscript:

> (*Stimulus*) "Nancy," the chairman said, "we have decided to make you a vice president of the firm!"
> (*Response*) "Oh no!" Nancy said. "How could I have such bad luck!"

Now, assuming Nancy is your normal, ambitious, go-getting central figure, this negative response to a wonderful stimulus makes no sense at all. The reader reading such a transaction will be puzzled, and will probably stop believing the story right at this point.

What went wrong? Of course: The internalization that would explain Nancy's strange response has been omitted. (It's amazing how often writers *assume* that the transaction is clear when it is as puzzling as this one.)

What to do? Put in the internalization that explains things, like this:

> (*Stimulus*) "Nancy," the chairman said, "we have decided to make you a vice president of the firm!"
>
> (*Internalization*) Nancy reeled with shock. She had come to this meeting expecting a demotion. Instead, they were offering her the job she had always dreamed of. But only an hour ago she had signed on with Acme Co., and could not go back on that contract. Just when she had everything she had ever wanted in her grasp, she had to leave Zilch Corp.
>
> (*Response*) "Oh no!" Nancy said. "How could I have such bad luck!"

As clumsy and obvious as I have made this illustration for the sake of clarity, you can see how the process works. In a moment we can look at a brief excerpt which provides more complex examples.

Before doing that, however, an additional point should be made.

It's possible that sometimes you the author might *want* the reader to be shocked and puzzled for a moment. You might want to create a surprising or even bizarre stimulus-response transaction as a means of creating momentary curiosity and/or suspense for the reader, planning to explain the internalization a few paragraphs or pages later. This is perfectly fine, but it's an advanced technique; the fact that it's done, sometimes for very special reasons, does not obviate the fact that stimulus, internalization and response ordinarily should be presented to the reader *in their natural order*. Writing them out of order can create big—or more subtle—problems.

Here's another simple example:

> Joe turned after hearing the gunshot.

What's wrong with that? Grammatically, nothing whatsoever.

But consider: What was the stimulus? What was the response? In what order does the sentence present them?

That's right. The sentence, in terms of stimulus and response, is backwards. It should read:

> Hearing the shot, Joe turned.

I hope you'll forgive me if I seem to beat this thing to death. Not only is a great deal of fiction-writing messed up at this very basic level; the principle of cause and effect, stimulus and response, lies at the heart of everything that follows in this book. As we shall see, you can't write modern fiction scenes unless you understand and practice proper cause and effect;

you can't link scenes together unless you understand the same principle; and you can't create a cohesive overall plot for your story or novel unless you can see the underlying dynamic of cause and effect which is at the heart of making your scenes not only link, but build with the kind of momentum and suspense that keeps readers worried — and fascinated.

Now, perhaps, we can turn to a more lengthy example which uses the basic stimulus-response techniques just discussed, but in a slightly more sophisticated way. The following is an edited excerpt from my latest novel involving a series character named Brad Smith. In this, part of chapter 35 of the novel titled *Double Fault*, we have just seen Brad being hit from behind and abducted from a motel-strip where his friend Collie Davis is also staying. The chapter changes to the viewpoint of Davis as he becomes aware of Brad's abduction and enters into a chase.

> Collie Davis hung up his cabin telephone. . . . Starting toward the door to give Brad the news, he heard (*Stimuli*) the sudden roar of a car engine being revved, then the nasty crunch of tires spinning in gravel. A sound like air gun pellets loudly peppered the front wall of his cabin.
>
> (*Response*) "Maniac," Davis muttered, cracking his front door to see who was playing destruction derby in the gravel parking area.
>
> (*Stimuli*) A late-model Buick sedan, filthy with road dust, most of the bodywork on its right side smashed and dented, was just pulling out of the motel parking area onto the blacktop pavement, heading south out of the cloud of pale yellow dust it had just created. One of its wheels spun an instant on the asphalt, howling.
>
> Davis got only a glimpse of the occupants, but it was enough. (*Immediate motivating stimulus*) Behind the wheel, a small bald man in a dark jacket. On the passenger side, slumped back against the seat's headrest, *Brad*.
>
> (*Internalization*) Unconscious or worse, judging by the way his head rolled to the side as the car veered fully onto the pavement and headed south.
>
> (*Response*) Davis ducked back into his cabin. It took him perhaps ten seconds to grab his Browning out of the compartment in his suitcase and scoop up his car keys off the rustic bedside table.
>
> Running outside to his rented Taurus, he glanced south and saw (*Additional stimulus-information*) that the Buick had already vanished around a slight turn in the highway where it started to ascend into the foothills. (*Response*) He grabbed his door handle and almost broke some fingers, forgetting he had locked up. (*Stimulus-response pattern reversed in the previous sentence to portray Davis's furious haste and confusion.*) Getting the key in the lock and jumping inside took another few precious seconds. Backing out seemed to take an eternity.
>
> (*More response*) Flooring the Taurus's accelerator, he swung onto the pavement and headed in the direction the Buick had taken. (*Response of onlookers to stimulus of Davis's speeding car is now given, but again in reverse of the normal order to add to impression of speed and confusion.*) Startled faces looked up from an open-air vegetable stand as he rocketed past them, the Ford's transmission screaming in protest at such violent treatment. (*Davis's seeing the startled faces is a new stimulus to him, and he has an internalization:*) All I need is for the town constable or somebody to arrest me for speeding, Davis thought.

(*Stimulus*) Reaching the curve where the Buick had vanished, (*Response*) he had to ease off a bit and allow the transmission to upshift. Then he poured power to the engine again, and it responded sweetly, the speedometer going up around 70.

(*Stimulus*) Ahead—well ahead, too far ahead—Davis could see the Buick nearing the outskirts of town, brake lights flaring brightly in the evening gloom, then swinging to the right and off the highway. (*Response*) He kept standing on the gas until he was almost on top of the place where the Buick had turned, seeing only at the last second that the intersecting road was gravel. (*Stimulus*) He swayed violently onto the gravel, half-losing it as the back end slewed around, (*Response*) then catching control again and pouring on more power. (*Stimulus*) The guy in the Buick with Brad had turned on his headlights, (*Response*) which made two nice red taillight signals for Davis to watch for. (*Character intention*) He kept his lights out to avoid detection if possible.

(*Series of stimuli*) The gravel road swung through a series of curves and came out in the deep canyon of a shallow river off to Davis's left. He was having a bad time seeing the road in the dimness without headlights. A pale cloud of whitish powder put in the air by the Buick ahead didn't help matters.

Sweat stung Davis's eyes. (*Internalization to complex of stimuli*) He was walking a tightrope, and knew it: get too close, and the bald man would realize he was being followed and possibly kill Brad—if he hadn't already done so; fall too far back in an overabundance of caution, on the other hand, and you could lose him altogether. Davis took several gravel curves in controlled drifts, and was rewarded with a glimpse of the Buick taillights well ahead. The bastard was driving like a maniac.

Which he probably was, Davis thought. Davis hadn't had time to see much, but he had seen enough to know that the driver of the car ahead fit the sketchy description he had of the conspirator who was still at large.

(*Character internalization continues, ruminating on other character's motivations—story causes behind his immediate action-stimuli*) What did he want with Brad? Revenge? If so, for what? Far more likely, he had learned somehow that Brad might know where Kevin Green was. But how could abducting Brad help the loony in any way—abduction being far and away the best Davis could assume this was?

Sheer red rock walls closed in tightly on the road, which had begun to get worse, narrower and washboarded by traffic and erosion. (*Stimulus*) Ahead was a tighter curve to the right around an outcropping of the hundred-foot rock face. (*Response*) Davis eased off a little and then swung wide into the turn. At the last possible instant (*Stimulus*) he spotted the yellow glare of headlights just around the bend somewhere. (*Response*) Jamming his weight hard on the brake, he spun the wheel and (*Stimulus*) felt for an instant that he was losing the Taurus altogether. . . .

Look at some of your own writing. Check very carefully to make sure that you are providing causes for desired effects, showing the effects of causes already in your copy. Look, too, at your smallest stimulus-response transactions:

- For every stimulus, do you show a response?
- For every response, have you provided an immediate, external stimulus?
- In complicated transactions, have you provided the reader with an explanatory internalization?
- Are the parts presented in the correct, textbook order, except when you *want* to connote confusion?

One final clarification. Throughout the part of this chapter dealing with stimulus and response, words like "external" and "physical" have been used with regularity. This was not an accident. Stimulus must be something on the stage in the story "now," something (as mentioned earlier) that could be seen or heard or otherwise perceived with the senses of the audience if you were to put the transaction on a theater stage. Responses, too, must be external — physical.

If you were to write either of the following transactions, you would be dead wrong, and missing the point:

> Having been angry for days, Joe punched Sam.

or:

> Rick hit Bill. Bill was surprised.

Why are these stimulus-response transactions faulty? Because in the first case *no stimulus was shown*. What was shown was internal — inside Joe's feelings, and it was not immediate; it was background that had been going on for quite some time. Joe was motivated by anger to hit Sam, but that doesn't explain specifically why he hit him right then and there. He had no immediate, physical, external stimulus. In the second case, Bill's surprise *is not a response* as we have defined response here; it is an internalization.

You may wish to go back and look again at the longer excerpt provided a bit earlier in this chapter. Note that — even in a wildly confusing sequence of events:

1. Nearly all the transactions are presented in the normal order.
2. Every transaction is completed — i.e., every stimulus brings on a response.
3. Internalization is caused by a stimulus; it doesn't "just happen."
4. Internalization is inserted in the proper order — after a stimulus and before the next response.
5. When transactions are presented out of their normal order, the effect on the reader is one of confusion.

It will be well for you to look hard at your own copy in these terms, too. If you find foggy logic, or get a bit confused in trying to repair obviously flawed transactions, try to think of *cause* as background or previously decided motivation; *effect* as the possibly complicated results of such background or motivation; *stimulus* as something much more immediate, in terms of time, and always in the outside world; *response* as also immediate and physical, and *internalization* as the process that goes on inside the receiver of a stimulus *after* that stimulus and *before* whatever response is to follow.

The more you work with this, the closer you will come to the first step in understanding scene and structure.

For one additional example of stimulus-response writing —

See Appendix 2.

CHAPTER 4

STRUCTURE IN LARGER ELEMENTS: THE SCENE

THE SCENE IS THE BASIC large building block of the structure of any long story. Just as cause and effect have a pattern, and stimulus and response form a fundamental unit of construction, the scene is the larger element of fiction with an internal structure just as unvarying, and rules just as vital to your ability to write dynamic fiction that makes sense and moves inexorably forward in a way readers find delightful.

Just as causes result in effects and stimuli result in responses, the scene inevitably—if written correctly—leads to another scene.

What is a scene? It's a segment of story action, written moment-by-moment, without summary, presented onstage in the story "now." It is *not* something that goes on inside a character's head; it is physical. It could be put on the theater stage and acted out.

What is the pattern of a scene? Fundamentally, it is:

- Statement of *goal*.
- Introduction and development of *conflict*.
- Failure of the character to reach his goal, a tactical *disaster*.

Readers generally find nothing as enthralling as conflict. Most popular novels, for example, are basically the record of a prolonged struggle. But as we mentioned in chapter 2, a story of any length must have some sort of movement or progress; you can't expect a reader to be patient very long with a story that drags out a single, unchanging conflict over many, many pages. You know the kind of static, unchanging conflict I mean; you see it when small children argue:

> Mary: "Mommy, make him stop! He hit me!"
> Billy: "I did not!"
> "Did so!"
> "Did not!"
> "Did so!"
> "Did not!"

"Did so!"
"Did not!"

Maybe the story question at the start of this little plot was: "Will Mary get mommy to make Billy stop?" And this question very quickly became: "Will Mary convince mommy in light of Billy's denial?" But that's as far as it got; Mary and Billy kept fighting about exactly the same issue, over and over and over again, *ad infinitum*.

Fusses like this drive mommies nuts.

If you have ever had the misfortune of witnessing an argument between partners in a failing marriage or troubled relationship, you may have seen another example of circular argument: Complaint brings on counter-complaint, which gets us nowhere, or one partner's statement may stimulate the other to say something like, "That's not what you're really thinking at all!"—which also gets nowhere in terms of a solution to anything.

Such circular nondevelopment of conflict in fiction drives readers nuts, too. Or, more likely, drives them away from your story.

How do you avoid such circularity in your fiction? By writing scenes.

THE GOAL

The scene, you see, has conflict at its heart, but is not static. It is a dynamic structural component with a definite internal pattern which forces the story to move forward as the scene plays—and as a result of its ending.

The prototypical scene begins with the most important character—invariably the viewpoint character—walking into a situation with a definite, clear-cut, specific *goal* which appears to be immediately attainable. This goal represents an important step in the character's game plan—something to be obtained or achieved which will move him one big step closer to attainment of his major story goal.

You will remember that stories start with a character jarred out of his sense of ease by a disturbing development of some kind that represents threatening change in the status quo. The character, we said then, forms an intention or long-term goal, the attainment of which will make things "right" again. The reader looks at this story goal statement and turns it into a long-term story question, so that the following type of dynamic takes place:

> (*Story goal*) "I must be first to climb that mountain!" Fred said.
> (*Reader's story question*) "Will Fred succeed in being first to climb the mountain?"

With the result that the reader reads avidly, seeking an answer to the story question you the author gave him to worry about when you showed Fred's goal.

Obviously you can't allow Fred to succeed—or fail totally—on page

2 of your planned book—because if you do, the story question has been answered on page 2 and your story has ended on page 2. Development of a story depends on your ability to interpose obstacles between your hero and the attainment of his goal. Most often, this interposition of obstacles is accomplished by putting someone in the story's cast who will provide live, ongoing opposition—a villain figure—who will be in constant *conflict* with the hero, either by trying to beat him up the mountain by hook or crook, or by thwarting the hero with the idea of keeping him from ever reaching his goal.

Well, you couldn't write a novel with Fred simply saying, over and over, that he wanted to be first, and Bart snarling repeatedly, "Oh, no, you're not!" The conflict has to be developed and it has to move somewhere.

How do you accomplish this? By developing a series of scenes.

The scene begins with a stated, clear-cut goal. Sometimes the character can carry over his clear-cut, immediate goal from the previous scene, and sometimes he can think it, going in. (Once every hundred scenes, maybe you can get away with allowing the goal to be implicit, as I did in the scene quoted in the last chapter where I thought it was rather obvious that Collie Davis set out to chase the other car.) But most of the time the character actually states his immediate scene goal in obvious, unmistakable fashion.

Let's assume for a moment that we are starting to write a novel using Fred's goal of wanting desperately to be first to climb the mountain. The reader now forms his story question. But the story has to start someplace, and it has to show dynamic forward movement.

Let's further assume, then, that Fred comes up with a game plan for his quest. He decides that his first step must be to borrow sufficient money to equip his expedition. So he walks into the Ninth District Bank of Cincinnati, sits down with Mr. Greenback, the loan officer, and boldly states his goal, thus:

> "Mr. Greenback, I want to be first to climb the mountain. But I must have capital to fund my expedition. Therefore I am here to convince you that you should lend me $75,000."

At this point, the reader sees clearly that this short-term goal relates importantly to the long-term story goal and the story question. So just as he formed a story question, the reader now forms a *scene question*, which again is a rewording of the goal statement: "*Will* Fred get the loan?"

Here is a note so important that I want to set it off typographically:

The scene question cannot be some vague, philosophical one such as, "Are bankers nice?" *or* "What motivates people like Fred?" *The question is specific, relates to a definite, immediate goal, and can be answered with a simple yes or no.*

Now: We've opened a potential scene. We have a character, we have a goal that relates to the story goal, and this short-term scene goal has been stated in no uncertain terms.

What next? It must be *conflict*.

Why? Not just because readers like conflict, but—again—because a prompt, satisfactory answer ends the scene at once and relaxes all tension in the reader. Let's imagine Mr. Greenback says, "I love mountain climbers, Fred, and I like you! Sure, you can have $75,000! But are you sure that will be enough? Are you sure you wouldn't like to borrow more?"

If you let this happen, the "scene" collapsed before it could get under way. Furthermore, Fred leaves happy and relaxed. The reader relaxes, too—and so loses interest in the story.

No. We can't have that. That's why we must develop conflict. And conflict—the give-and-take between two characters—will make up 95 to 98 percent of the length of the scene. Mr. Greenback cannot under any circumstances jovially agree to let Fred have the money at once. He must instead announce his opposition to the expedition right at the outset, and may even be openly hostile to Fred as a person.

He and Fred, in other words, have to fight.

Such scene fights are the be-all and end-all for lovers of fiction. Readers enjoy watching the antagonists punch and counterpunch. They love sweating bullets with the hero as he struggles for the upper hand. They get their excitement in the scenes—*they like to live them in their imagination.*

This being the case, you want to build your scenes as big as possible, and you want to make them just as believable—as lifelike—as you possibly can. The most important way you attain this end is by presenting each scene *moment by moment,* leaving nothing out, because there is no summary in real life, and you can't have any summary in the scene, either, if you are shooting for maximum lifelikeness and reader involvement.

And how do you structure this large, vital conflict portion of the scene to make it moment by moment? You do so by carefully following the rules of stimulus and response as outlined in chapter 3.

So Fred enters the bank and tells Mr. Greenback his immediate goal. The reader forms this into a scene question, and then is enthralled as he watches Fred and the banker argue, counterpunch, voice objections, and marshal answers to the objections, and so on.

This particular scene in the bank will probably be almost entirely dialogue, with just enough gesture, facial expression, etc., thrown in to keep the reader physically oriented in his imagination. (Most scenes have dialogue in them—argument—but other types of scenes exist. Imagine a scene with no dialogue in it at all, one in which our heroine fights to keep her car on the road as the driver of another car keeps ramming her from behind and pulling up alongside, trying to edge her over the embankment.)

So far, so good. But every scene (like all other good things) must come to an end. We don't want this argument in the bank to run 350 pages! So how should it end? As said before, with a tactical *disaster.*

ENDING THE SCENE

"Disaster" in this usage does not often denote an earthquake, a flood, a plane crash, or anything like the things we often term disasters in real life. But use of the term is justified because the character—and the reader—experience the final twist in a scene as thoroughly bad—disastrous to the attainment of the immediate scene goal, and so a terrible setback in the quest for the story goal.

It seems clear why this should be so. If a character enters a scene, has a big struggle, and comes out with exactly what he went in for, then he is happy as a lark. Again—just as if there had been no fight at all—Fred is happy, the reader is happy—and all story tension just went down the drain.

This is why the scene, if it is to work as a building block in your novel, must end not well, but badly. Fred cannot be allowed to attain his scene goal. He must encounter a new setback. *He must leave in worse shape than he was when he went in.* Any time you can build a scene which leaves your character in worse shape, you have probably "made progress" in terms of your story's development!

In terms of the scene question, in other words, you cannot allow the answer to be a simple "yes!" Whatever the character wanted—whatever the scene question—the answer must be negative.

A simple "no!" may suffice. Returning to our example, Fred may be told after all his arguments and conflict with the banker that he simply will not receive a loan. When Fred walks out of the bank, he has been set back and is in worse shape than he was when he entered, because he has tried to take one of his hoped-for steps toward climbing the mountain, and has been rebuffed. At the very least, he has lost one option.

The banker might also, however, thwart Fred—and provide us with a disaster—in another way. He might give Fred a "yes!" answer, but one with so many strings attached that Fred can't accept it.

For example, Mr. Greenback might say, "Well, Fred, all right. You can have your loan. *But* you must agree to pay 60 percent interest, you must deed your automobile to us, and you must sell your mother's house and put her in a nursing home so we can be assured that you won't be messing around trying to help her when you're supposed to be climbing that mountain."

Such *"Yes, but"* disasters are often better than a simple "No!" because they put the hero on the horns of a moral dilemma, and in making an ethical choice to turn down the crummy deal, he in effect brings on his own disaster. (Of such stuff are heroes often made.)

In addition, the banker could provide Fred with a *"No, and furthermore!"* disaster at the end of the scene. In such a case, the banker might finally lose patience with Fred's insistence that the mountain-climbing expedition is vital, and tell him something like, "Fred, you have tried my patience beyond endurance. I am now convinced that you are not only pushy, but dangerously obsessed. My answer is *no, and furthermore*, we are calling in the small note you already owe us. Pay up or go to jail!"

Obviously I've used a farfetched example here for purposes of exaggerated illustration. But as you study popular fiction in the days and weeks ahead, notice how often the scenes indeed do end with something more complex than a simple "No!" disaster—how the writer skillfully turned events at the ending of the scene so that the character quite clearly left the scene in far worse shape than if he had never entered the scene and tried. This kind of development not only tightens reader tension and increases reader worry, it also tends to build reader sympathy for the viewpoint character, who planned so well and fought so hard—only to be swatted down once more.

Whatever type of disaster you concoct for your scene ending, however, please note that it must answer the scene question and none other. You cannot get by with a disaster that says to the reader, in effect, "Well, I don't know if Fred got the money, but he had a coughing fit." *Or:* "Did Fred get the money? I don't know; but he sure left the office depressed." *Or:* "Did he get the money? Who knows? But there was an earthquake!"

This simply won't do. You have to play fair with your reader. You stated a character goal, and the reader formed a scene question. Your disaster must answer the question that was posed.

Note further, if you please, that this answer must be a development which grows logically yet to some degree unexpectedly out of the conflict. If Fred and Mr. Greenback argue about whether Fred should get his loan, and in the course of the argument get off on environmental issues almost exclusively, then Mr. Greenback's disastrous decision at the end of the scene must be based at least in part on some environmental question. You can't have them fight about one thing, and then just stick on a disaster which doesn't fit. You can't end a scene about money with an earthquake, a heart attack, a tornado, a fire, or any other gratuitous "bad thing" just because it might be termed a disaster. Always remember the specialized kind of disaster we're talking about here: *an unanticipated but logical development that answers the scene question, relates to the conflict that has been presented, and sets the character back.*

SCENE LENGTH

Now a word about length: How long should a scene be?

There is no simple answer. You have already noted, I am sure, that the statement of the scene goal will ordinarily be very brief, seldom more than a few lines. Even if the viewpoint character reiterates the scene goal several times during the conflict portion of the segment, all the total wordage directly specifying the scene goal will be quite small. The disaster, too, often comes in a very few words—a cannonade fired at the very end of the scene, and seldom more than a hundred words in length.

This leaves the inescapable fact that the length of any scene will depend largely on the extent to which you the author develop the conflict section — how long you write it.

We've already seen that you can't write it in a repetitious, circular, "Did so! — Did not!" fashion and hold reader interest. Just as the ground on which the story stands is constantly shifting, the ground under the scene shifts in the same way. On page 3 of a scene, for example, the characters should not be arguing about *precisely* the same factors they began with; someone should have offered a new line of argument. And if the scene goes on through another several pages, the persons in conflict should continually be shifting their tactics, changing their approach, trying different lines of logic, etc.

None of this tells you how long a given scene should be, of course. A general rule might suggest that the length of the scene should be directly proportional to its importance in the overall plot. Thus Fred's scene with the banker — vital as it may be — probably should be shorter in the final story than a later scene in which Fred and a competitive climber struggle for momentary possession of a rocky shelf halfway up the mountain — the loser likely to lose not only the race, but his life. The higher the stakes, the longer the scene.

As recently as a decade ago, scenes extending ten or more book pages were not uncommon. Perhaps due to the kind of reader impatience noted earlier in this book (or perhaps because publishers these days lean on writers to produce tighter, shorter books that can be published with lower financial investment up front), a trend has developed toward shorter scenes — ones that may not develop *all* possible angles of conflict.

Today's "fully developed scene," consequently, tends to run shorter than it once did. You may encounter scene situations where you simply can't develop all the complex immediate issues in fewer than a dozen pages. If so, that's fine. But I suspect that the average, "developed" print-fiction scene today runs between four and six pages, and some are shorter than that.

If you have serious doubts about how long a given scene should be, I think your best course would be to write it for all you think it might possibly be worth. Novels that a publisher considers too long — but are excellent in all other respects — will usually attract an editor's invitation to "boil." But the scene you underdeveloped — so that it lost its potential dramatic punch — will not get the publisher's attention at all, and your manuscript will simply be rejected. In my own teaching experience, fifty manuscripts fail because of scenic underdevelopment for every one that fails because the scenes were written too long.

Finally, although the point has been stated repeatedly and implied even more often, it's well to emphasize a point that invariably is asked during lectures on the subject of scene structure and its essential component, the conflict.

The question: "Do I have to have the conflict outside the character? Can't I have the character at war with himself inside his head?"

Answer: The conflict has to be on the outside. If you remember the example of writing something which could be put on the theater stage, you will not forget this principle.

Of course there will also be conflict inside the character. Ideally, the conflict taking place on the stage now, in this scene, will dovetail nicely with whatever internal conflict the character is experiencing—and will make it a lot worse. But readers can't be lectured about internal conflict that doesn't show—doesn't "play" dramatically—and so can't be seen. In the scene portions of your story, Fred can be going through a hell of internal torment and in all kinds of conflict with himself. He *should* be. But in the scene that's not where you focus. You focus *outside*, not in.

If you have not been writing with full awareness of scene structure, let me urge you to practice planning a number of scenes strictly as an exercise. Always start with a goal, plan your conflict, and devise a solid disaster. If you can't quickly come up with a list of possible scene goals of your own, you might want to try the following, in each case writing at least three paragraphs outlining the nature of the opposition and some of the key steps in the conflict, and then specifying a good disaster that might usefully end that scene.

Here is your working practice list:

1. Accused of cheating on a test, Janis goes to visit her math professor with the *goal* of convincing him she did not cheat.

2. Searching for an embezzler, Calvin accosts the bank examiner with the *goal* of convincing the examiner to give him the name of the prime suspect.

3. Lost in the caverns, Billy explores a narrow shaft with the *goal* of finding his way out. (A hard one! No living opponent.)

4. Ted visits Jennifer with the *goal* of getting her to marry him.

5. Wanting to win permission to enter graduate school, Bari goes into the office of the graduate dean with the *goal* of convincing him to let her in. (If the dean is a male, there is a very obvious *"Yes, but!"* disaster possibility lurking at the end of this scene.)

See Appendix 3.

CHAPTER 5

STRUCTURE IN MACROCOSM: SCENES WITH RESULTS

THE GOOD, EFFECTIVE FICTION SCENE will have results. That seems pretty obvious: A fight ending in a disastrous setback changes the situation in which the story is playing out, and nothing will ever be quite the same again.

In devising your scenes, however, it's important to consider scene goals, angles in the conflict, and the nature of the disaster you impose at the end of the scene—all in terms of *scope* of result, *immediacy* of result, *finality* of result, and *direction* of result. Conflict usually causes pain, and disasters usually cause significant changes in the course of the plot. But it's possible to have too much of a good thing, just as it is to have not enough of a bad thing.

All of us yearn as writers for grand scene goals, powerful conflict, and gloriously terrible disasters. But we all have to plan carefully lest we write ourselves up some blind alley. Let's consider first scene *goal* and how the goal, if selected badly for a scene, might bring us to grief in terms of the ultimate results of the scene.

GOAL SELECTION

In terms of the scope of the result of the scene to be written, a writer can err in two possible ways: She can select a goal so small or insignificant that the scope of the result cannot possibly be broad enough to affect the course of the story, or she can select a goal so gigantic and all-encompassing that the scope of the scene result will be earth-shattering—probably ending the story right then and there, or possibly changing the course of the rest of the story so drastically that the main character may never again have a realistic chance.

Fred Redux

How could you err by giving Fred, the mountain climber, a scene goal too insignificant to have measurable results in terms of a later disaster?

Suppose you decide that he chooses as his first scene goal the procure-ment of a good pair of climbing boots. (Scene question: *Will* Fred get good boots?) Leaving aside the obvious fact that few readers in their right mind will be willing to worry much about such a petty matter, suppose you develop a scene around this goal anyway. How much meaningful scope can possibly come at the end of such a scene?

Maybe Fred learns that there simply aren't any boots made that are as good as the ones he has envisioned (a "No!" disaster). Or maybe Fred learns that the kind of boot he really wants is so expensive that he'll have to borrow a few hundred dollars—or work overtime a few nights—to be able to afford them (a "Yes, but!" disaster). Maybe he even learns that they don't make boots to fit his oddly shaped foot, and sprains his big toe trying to fit himself into an ill-fitting pair that happens to be available (a "No, and furthermore!" disaster).

Big deal! *So what?* Who cares? How has such a "disastrous" result really made things significantly tougher for Fred? The goal was too small, the scope of the result too narrow. The story has bogged down to a virtual standstill.

Now imagine trying to start over with a terrifically more important scene goal. Is it possible to select a goal that's too vast in scope? Oh, yes.

Imagine that we let out all the stops and decide that Fred's first step, on his way to the mountain of his dreams, is to go on a local television talk show and convince the interviewer—a notorious cynic—that local people should contribute money to his climbing expedition for the sake of civic pride; his goal is to get his needed financial backing through this TV appearance, or else.

Going in with this great goal, Fred encounters hostility and barbs from the show host, and at the end loses his temper, is laughed at, and becomes such a laughingstock in the community that not only will he not receive any financial help, but some members of his family start thinking seriously about having him committed for long-term psychiatric care.

This is a great disaster, all right, but by setting up a scene goal of such massive scope—by allowing Fred to put all his eggs in one basket—we have doomed ourselves to a scene disaster of such enormous scope that he can never recover. *We have doomed his quest.*

We must always be on the lookout for scene goals that are too small to allow for sufficient scope of disaster. Just as obviously, we must guard against allowing our heroes to pick goals of such magnitude that the scope of scene disaster will destroy them.

Another goal-selection error can be found in picking a goal which cannot logically lead to a scene-ending result with any immediacy. The careful writer of fiction wants the disaster which grows out of the goal to put considerable additional pressure on the character very soon. If you allow Fred, for example, to pick a scene goal of convincing the Smithson-ian Institution to fund his expedition, it could well lead to a "disaster" in which some Washington official says *"Yes, but"* such requests have to be formally approved by a board which meets only twice a year—thus mean-ing that the result of this disaster is a waiting period of several months.

Or—and this is a much more common mistake—you might err by failing to have Fred note at the outset, in stating his goal, that he needs a decision or declaration right away; in such cases, disasters have a tendency to look more like indefinite delays—and again the story bogs down because the goal was not set up or stated in such a way that a fairly immediate result could be forthcoming.

It's also possible to select goals which will result in scenic outcomes with *too much* immediacy. You've perhaps seen published books where this problem caused pacing too hectic to be believed. Going into the warehouse, gun in hand, with the intent to do or die, hero George gets shot at, almost run down by a car, and then mistakenly arrested for improper entry. He then runs for it—one disaster following another with machine-gun rapidity, so that he never has time to think or plan at all.

Ideally, a goal will be picked which will have immediate results, but not so horribly immediate and pressing that the character won't have time to draw a few breaths.

As to finality of result, it's good to remember that you can err by setting up a scene goal for which a disastrous ending may be *too* final. If your detective George enters a scene with the goal of kill or be killed, the chances are quite good that his disaster will be—being killed. Where do you go after you've killed your central character? (I think the book just ended!)

The reverse of this coin must be considered, too. It's cheating—and the reader won't like it a bit—if you set up a goal which will lead to an outcome that isn't final at all. We can return to our friend Fred for one example. Let's suppose he enters the bank, wanting his loan, but we take note of the fact that there are five banks in town, and this is just the first one. *Now* after he is turned down, the disaster isn't final at all; it's just a momentary setback, and he has four more banks to try.

Readers get irritated fast when they are asked to read scenes like this, where the disaster isn't really final—and therefore serious at all.

Finally, in terms of scene goals, it's important always to keep in mind the general direction in which you the author want the story to go after this particular scene. If you're intent on writing a mountain-climbing story, you *don't* have Fred go in for the bank loan, telling himself that if he fails to get the loan, he's going to go get a gun and rob the joint. The result of such an ill-advised plan at the outset of the scene will force Fred to turn bank robber after the disaster ending this scene—and we wanted to write a story about mountain climbing (not bank robbery), remember???

ANGLES IN THE CONFLICT

Once you have avoided the pitfalls inherent in planning scene goals, you enter the dark and scary jungle of the conflict portion of the scene—a place where efforts to build the tension can sometimes result in various miscues. This danger exists primarily because of the writer's wholly laudable desire to intensify the conflict in every scene as much as seems reasonable, and to diversify the grounds on which the conflict is based.

Just as a whole story can't be written in a boring, repetitious "Did So!—Did Not!" circle, the conflict portion of the scene can't be a seemingly endless repetition of exactly the same statements, either. The opponents must circle and feint, dodge and parry, try different arguments or strategies, think they're gaining and then fear they're losing, escalate their efforts, and so on. This is all to the good unless you the author get so carried away that you lose control of what's going on, with the result that the potential for conflict at the opening of the scene gets overrun in such a way that we no longer have battle #6, for example, but all-out Armageddon.

The converse is also sometimes true. Sensing, perhaps, that a particular angle developed in the conflict portion would be extremely difficult to write—or perhaps even personally painful to deal with—the writer may sometimes ignore or block out potentially useful angles that the conflict might take. In such cases, all the possible excesses of result that could follow overdoing the conflict are reversed—and the conflict is so watered down that little can possibly result from any conceivable disaster that could grow logically out of the scene struggle.

It's easy to see how either of these miscues can happen, causing bad things in terms of scope of scene results, immediacy of result, finality of result, or direction of result.

Let's look first at what happens when you go overboard and make the conflict *too* vicious or strong.

The Strongman

In terms of our friend Fred, the mountain climber, suppose you sense a weakness in the conflict portion as he and the banker argue about a possible loan; your goal statement was fine: *"I must get a loan to fund my expedition."* But now in the conflict portion you feel uneasy, think the argument may be starting to be repetitious, and so you escalate.

"What if," you say to yourself, "Mr. Greenback starts attacking Fred's business background, and Fred angrily hurls onto the table his home mortgage and papers for an existing loan made to his company?" (With this escalation, you figure, the conflict will toughen up.)

It's highly possible that the escalation would indeed make the conflict sharper and more interesting. It's even logical that such an escalation could take place, growing out of a goal statement that didn't necessarily promise such huge single-scene stakes. But throwing so many blue chips on the table carries with it the danger that the disaster which must now grow out of such an escalation could have greater scope than you desired early in your story; it's possible that Fred could leave the bank not only *sans* his desired loan, but with his company loan called in for immediate payment and his home mortgage in jeopardy. And maybe that's a disaster with considerably broader scope than you intended when you started to write this scene! Occasionally such a "surprise" may stimulate you to heighten tension throughout the rest of the story; usually, however, you're in danger of losing control of both the direction and pace of your story.

In like manner, overdoing it in an effort to bolster a scene's conflict can bring on results that are *too* immediate. Fred may—as an escalation of the conflict—demand to see the bank president, for example. This may look like a good development as the "inspiration" flits into your mind. But such an intensification could result not only in his failure to see the president, but in his being thrown out of the bank, branded a kook, made the subject of telephone calls to other lenders warning that a madman is on the loose, etc. Given such bad and *immediate* results, Fred might have no time to plan a new course of action—might be virtually wiped out instantly.

Overintensification of the conflict, or introduction of a wrong angle, can also have an adverse effect on the finality of the result. If, for example, in building the conflict, you decide to try a more physical angle to the fight—and have Fred lose his temper and punch out Mr. Greenback—Fred is almost certainly going to play his next scene in jail, and has a trial date; his quest for the mountain has almost surely been lost—period!—right now.

And how can overintensification or selection of a wrong angle result in a bad direction at the end of the scene? This is perhaps the most common mistake made by new writers in creating scenes, and it goes of course to the larger problem of plot planning.

Suppose you decide somewhere in the course of the conflict portion of the scene in the bank to have Fred start arguing that he can always borrow the money in New York, but he doesn't want to go that far from home. Mr. Greenback can interpret this as an insult or a threat, and the fight can sharpen. But once Fred has introduced the New York angle, you the author will be forced to follow up on it if this scene ends in disaster—as it must. So you suddenly find yourself one or two scenes following Fred into the lobby of Chase Manhattan—all because you escalated by putting a wrong angle into the conflict in the earlier scene.

(It's this kind of scene-handling error, incidentally, that usually can be found in the work of a novelist who complains about losing her way in the plot. Sometimes they even say something like, "I don't know what's happened! My characters have just taken over the story!" Characters don't take over stories! Characters don't exist except in your imagination. When you think a character has taken your story off in the wrong direction, it's likely that the real culprit is your failure in technique—the introduction of a potentially damaging angle in the conflict part of the scene. There are a couple of other places where you can inadvertently send your story off on the wrong vector, and we'll get to those also in due time.)

So efforts to "build up" a particular scene can have awful effects on the nature of the disaster to follow, with even worse results later in the plot. But conflict sections that are too soft or weak—ones in which the author makes a move to *duck* or tone down conflict, for whatever reason, can be just as bad.

Ninety-Eight-Pound Weakling

Now that you see clearly what I'm talking about here, it doesn't seem necessary to go through every type of impact that weakening or diluting a scene's conflict portion might have. I think you can see clearly that conflict that is too weak, or over an issue that's insignificant, can hardly be expected to lead to a logical disaster that's very big in terms of scope, immediacy, finality or direction. The writer who makes a move (selects angles in her scene development) which weaken or duck the conflict is a writer whose disasters can never credibly be very disastrous. And if she does happen to come up with a decent (i.e., difficult) disaster growing out of weak conflict, it won't likely be the time that puts pressure on the hero to do anything anytime soon.

Why would a writer dilute the conflict or even duck it altogether? Every so often, she might do it intentionally to "ease off" on the reader, momentarily slowing the story for a desired effect. But here I am talking about unrealized, unconscious easing off. This is almost always a bad thing, and there seem to be three possible reasons for it to happen: shyness, fear or fatigue.

I've used the word "shyness" to describe one reason a writer might dodge or water down the conflict part of a scene, but I'm not entirely happy with the choice of that word. It's just the best I can come up with. What I'm referring to is the fact that most of us try to dodge or soften conflict in real life, and many of us find that even the writing of strong conflict is a bit painful since we are not, after all, violent people. So some writers weaken their conflict portions without realizing it because they're so "nice."

Fear may also cause one to dilute the conflict or pick weak angles of development for it. In such cases the writer may see clearly the direction she should go, and she may even realize that her conflict is weak. But, "I could never write well enough to portray such a fight!" she'll say. Or, "I see that there should be a car chase here, but I don't describe things well enough to handle that, so I just had Fred pull over voluntarily."

One of the finest writers I ever coached had such a fear problem. She was so unsure of herself and her ability to write of powerful conflict that she went to amazing lengths to "write around" such segments she had imagined and plotted *as vital to her story*. For example, in one case I remember, she drove the plot relentlessly, through cause and effect, to a scene where the hero had to enter a business office and confront a powerful magnate with a demand that he relinquish control of a subsidiary company. A chapter ended with the hero walking into the building, and I turned the manuscript page, eager to read about the fight that was clearly at hand. The next chapter began with words very much like, *"After the showdown with Jacob Simms, David drove directly home, feeling. . . ."* Because she was afraid of her ability to write the big scene well, she had skipped it entirely!

Writers with such fears *must* force themselves to develop their conflict in face of the fear. If you are such a one, you will find that boldly going ahead into the "impossibly difficult" conflict portion will stretch your abilities as a writer—and make you better than you thought you could ever be.

In the writing of a long book, the writer may also simply fall victim to fatigue. Writing a big scene—vicariously experiencing all the strong emotions and then struggling to get them onto paper in the most effective way—is a tiring, draining process. The result of such fatigue, if not recognized, may be the production of scenes later in a manuscript which simply do not have full possible development because the writer was *tired*—physically, intellectually, emotionally.

If you ever find yourself feeling such fatigue—and suspect that it might be diluting your scene-writing—there is only one possible solution: a brief rest away from the manuscript. For one writer, sufficient rest might come from an afternoon of golf, while another might need to take a week off while she works on entirely unrelated problems at her accounting firm. Each writer must determine for herself if and when she gets overtired, and how she will rest herself.

NATURE OF THE DISASTER

You can see at this point that goals you pick for a scene, and how you handle the conflict portion, have a direct impact on the disaster at the end of the scene. But picking perfect goals and developing all the correct, intense angles of the conflict section do not necessarily guarantee that your scene-ending disaster will be "just right" also. It's possible to make every creative move perfectly up to the moment of the disaster—and then fall flat on your face.

Suppose you find, somewhere in the development of your plot, that "things have suddenly gone wrong." Don't—as already mentioned—imagine that the characters have taken over, that inspiration has failed you, or that it was all a bad idea to start with. Instead, work backward in the pages you have produced and examine each disaster that has befallen your hero at the end of each scene. At some point you will find a disaster that made the scope of all to follow either too large or too insignificant; made the results of the disaster too immediate or not pressing and immediate enough; caused a result that was too final (or not a significant change at all); or of a type that sent the story line off on a wrong vector that your original plot didn't foresee.

As implied in everything that has gone before in this chapter, you may at such a point have to go back and examine the kind of goal you set up for that erroneous scene, and if that doesn't show where you went wrong, you may have to analyze the steps you put into the conflict in an attempt to spot where you made a wrong move that foreordained the wrong kind of disaster. If you find any such error, of course you must fix it. But what if these parts of every scene seem fine, and you're still off course?

In such a case, it's likely that you wrote a good scene, but then slipped at the very end — tacking on the wrong kind of disaster.

Disaster, you will remember, must follow logically out of the stated goal, and grow logically but unexpectedly out of the conflict which grew out of the stated goal. A common structural problem in devising scene-ending disasters is failure by the author to consider the inevitable later plot results if a particular logical, unanticipated and generally acceptable disaster is selected to end the scene.

To put this another way, errors of *scope, immediacy and finality* usually come about because something went wrong in the goal or conflict portions of the scene. Errors of *direction* of result usually happen because something went wrong in precisely how the disaster was presented at the end of the scene.

Let me provide just one or two outlandish examples, and again — for the last time, I promise — we can use Fred as our illustration.

Let's say you've had Fred go in to try to get his loan, then have a stirring, just-right tiff with the banker. Now, seeking a good disaster with which to end the scene, you decide to have the banker say, "Fred, *yes* you can have your loan, *but* you must first climb Pikes Peak to prove to me that you are capable of this major expedition to Nepal." This is perfectly fine except in terms of story direction; such a disaster is going to send Fred to Colorado, and a climb up Pikes Peak, *and you didn't intend that to be in the story at all.* Obviously, what you have to do in this case is go back and tinker with the disaster, making Mr. Greenback say something else.

Or imagine for a moment that you still have a fine goal statement and excellent conflict development in the scene, but for a disaster you decide to have Fred fight so hard — and get so angry — that he has a heart attack. This is a grand disaster, all right — but such a disaster has headed your story in the direction of the hospital.

Of such thoughtless inspirations are lost stories made. But they can almost always be fixed, once you identify the single disaster-error that sent things reeling off in the wrong direction.

I had a clear demonstration of this fact some years ago when I wrote a novel centered on a murder mystery. Halfway through the book, my hero met a disaster which forced him to leave town — we'll call it Center-ville — and go off to another state in search of new evidence. I thought the book was fine, but when I sent it in, my editor sent it back at once with a curt rejection slip.

I called him. "What's wrong with it?" I asked.

"The story is just fine," he told me, "until Richard leaves Centerville. After that, the story never seems quite right again because you've lost all your local color."

Brooding about this, it dawned on me that my editor was (as usual) quite right about there being something wrong with the book. Looking back through the manuscript, I found a crucial scene just before my hero left town. In that scene, halfway through the book, my hero sought out a friend and struggled through a long conversation with him, trying to get him to give the name of someone previously seen near the murder site.

As written, the disaster was, in effect, "The man I saw was George, but he isn't in town anymore, and I don't know where he went."

This was fine, structurally. *Goal*: Learn who was near. (Scene question: *Will* hero learn who was near?) *Conflict*: Informant doesn't want to tell. *Disaster*: *Yes*, hero learns it was George, *but* now he has to go off elsewhere and search for George.

It immediately became clear at this point in my analysis that all I had to do was change the nature of the disaster. Simplicity itself: Hero asks friend for information, just as before. But the new disaster: "*Yes*, Mr. Hero, I know who was near the murder site, *but* it was the son of the mayor, and you will never be able to pin anything on such a prominent person."

I called my editor back. "You don't like the last part where he leaves town?" I asked.

"That's right," the editor said.

"Okay," I said. "Then I'll fix it so he never leaves town."

"My God!" my editor said. "Why didn't I think of that?"

Of course in this case the last half of the novel had to be extensively rewritten. But much of the action that had previously taken place somewhere else transferred very nicely to the new circumstances which logically followed *the changing of a single disaster* midway in the manuscript.

Although several later chapters will go into greater detail about the structure and content of scenes, and how they fit into a larger pattern, you have been given quite enough here to allow yourself considerable study of your own work to assure that you are writing basically sound scenes. Let me urge you to go through your work and mark the scene-opening goal statement in *red*, the conflict portion in *blue*, and the disaster in *black*. Then, with other colors, go back through the conflict section and underline in a different color each subtle shift of argument or change in tactics you can identify.

Having done all this, go back through yet another time and circle in some additional color *every time you have allowed your hero to repeat or reiterate his scene goal*. If you have kept things on the track, even a complicated scene with many shifts in the argument will find the hero trying doggedly on several occasions to repeat what he's here for. (This keeps him a bit on the track, and it doesn't hurt the reader's continuing sense of focus on the scene question, either.)

There will be more about repetition of the scene goal in chapter 10.

Finally, whether you work on a story you have on the drafting table or do it strictly as an exercise, please take at least a half dozen 5 × 7 file cards and plan some scenes.

At the top of each card, write the word *Goal* and then fill out in ten words or less what your central character wants in this scene.

Two lines below, write the word *Conflict* and write down *who* the conflict is to be with, *where* the conflict is to take place, *how long* in story time the conflict is to last, and *at least four twists or turns* that the conflict is to take during its playing out.

Near the bottom of the card, write the word *Disaster*. Write down what the disaster would be for this scene.

These working cards do not have to link. They can, in other words, be isolated imagined scenes from as many different possible novels. But if you can make some of them hook together, one behind the other in a cause-and-effect fashion, so much the better. For that's what you do when you *plot*.

CHAPTER 6

PLANNING AND REVISING SCENES FOR MAXIMUM EFFECT

WHEN I WAS A CHILD, longer ago than I like to admit, there was a children's storybook tale that never ceased to fascinate me. It was the story of the old woman and the pig.

The old woman, it seemed, went to market one day and bought a fine, live pig. Walking homeward, with the pig on a leash, she came upon a fence across her route. There was a ladder-like contraption—a stile—built to help one climb over the fence. But the pig was too large for the woman to pick up and carry over.

"Pig, pig," the old woman said. "Jump over the stile or I won't get home tonight." But the pig wouldn't.

Looking around in search of help, the old woman saw a dog nearby.

"Dog, dog," she said. "Bite pig. The pig won't jump over the stile, and I won't get home tonight." But the dog wouldn't.

Looking further, the old woman spied a stick.

"Stick, stick, beat dog," she implored. "Dog won't bite pig, pig won't jump over the stile, and I won't get home tonight." But the stick wouldn't.

Still looking for help, the old woman came upon a fire.

"Fire, fire," she said, "burn stick! Stick won't beat dog, dog won't bite pig, pig won't jump over the stile, and I won't get home tonight." But the fire wouldn't.

The old woman was not a quitter. She had her story goal—to get home—and I the reader had my story question: *Would* she get home that night? So she kept moving along intent on her story goal, and soon came to a pool of water.

"Water, water, quench fire," she urged. "Fire won't burn stick, stick won't beat dog, dog won't bite pig, pig won't jump over the stile, and I won't get home tonight!" But—you guessed it—the water wouldn't.

So—but you've begun to get the idea, I'm sure.

As a small child, I was not only fascinated with this story, but can still recall a certain degree of worry and tension in me as my mother read the tale to me over and over again. It was only *many* years later that it dawned on me that the story worked because all the scenes worked so well, all relating very clearly to the story question, and all ending in a disaster. (The pattern was too predictable for adult fiction—all simple "No!" disasters ending every scene, but it was just fine for a two year old.)

What does this have to do with planning and revising scenes for maximum effect? Actually, quite a lot. It illustrates several points that you the author must bear in mind when you're planning or revising in terms of scene structure and their linkages:

1. The goal of each scene must clearly relate to the story question in some way.

2. The conflict must be about the goal.

3. The conflict must be with another person or persons, not internally, within oneself.

4. Once a viewpoint has been established and that viewpoint character's problem and goal have been stated, it's wise to remain with that same, single viewpoint through the disaster.

5. Disaster works (moves the story *forward*) by seeming to move the central figure *further back* from his goal, leaving him in worse trouble than he was before the scene started.

6. Readers will put up with a lot if your scenes will only keep making things worse!

7. You can seldom, if ever plan, write, or revise a scene in isolation of your other plans for your story, because the end of each scene dictates a lot about what can happen later.

We've earlier discussed points 1, 2 and 3 above. They are listed again for additional emphasis. The moment a reader can't see the relevance to the story question of whatever is stated as a scene goal, the reader almost surely will yawn and lose interest in that upcoming scene. The moment the conflict in the scene turns so far from the stated scene goal that relevance is no longer imaginable, the reader will throw your story against the wall in irritated confusion. The moment the conflict goes "all inside," with nothing happening outside the character's mind, the very essence of scene—onstage conflict—is lost, and the reader will go to sleep.

Points 4 through 7, above, merit greater discussion. To repeat:

4. Once a viewpoint has been established and that viewpoint character's problem and goal have been stated, it's wise to remain with that same, single viewpoint through the disaster.

A thoroughgoing analysis of viewpoint as a fiction technique is beyond the scope of this book. I feel confident you already understand a lot about viewpoint, or my earlier somewhat casual mentions of the technique would have put you off before you got this far. But at the risk of being repetitious, let's just say once again that viewpoint is the technique by which the author picks a character inside the story, then tells the story from that person's view, so that the reader sees, hears, feels, and knows only what that viewpoint character can experience. Of course it's possible to have a so-called omniscient viewpoint, where the reader is made privy to the sense impressions, feelings and thoughts of virtually everyone in the story, but it's a terribly difficult way to write, and not very popular today. After all, each of us lives his or her life in a single viewpoint, so why not tell the story the same way?

Of course in long stories, especially modern novels, the author may decide to show the reader the viewpoint of several characters. It's not often, however, that you see the author jumping continuously from the head and heart of one character to the head and heart of another. Even novelists who write "multiple viewpoint" stories seldom jump the viewpoint around every paragraph or two. Most choose to limit the viewpoint in any given scene *to a single character in that scene* — invariably the character with the strongest, clearest goal motivation going in. To say this a different way: The goal that starts a scene ordinarily should be stated by the story person who is to be the viewpoint character in that scene. And once this viewpoint has been established, you will be wise to stay in that viewpoint at least through the disaster ending the scene.

Why should this be so? For one thing, your reader will tend strongly to identify with, and sympathize with, whatever character you make the viewpoint character. So if you have Bobbie open the scene with a statement of a goal, you should usually establish her as the viewpoint character at the same time because by so doing you will instantly help your reader decide whose side to take in the conflict that lies just ahead.

Another reason for giving the starting scene goal to the viewpoint character is the fact that you can better keep track of the goal — and how things are going — if you can slip into the viewpoint character's head every once in a while, as the scene goes along, to remind the reader what the scene goal is, and provide the reader with some indication of how the lead character thinks things are going at this point.

"But," I can almost hear you protesting, "if the conflict is supposed to be external, and not inside the character's head, how can I get into that character's head to show how he thinks things are going?" That's a good question, but if you will reflect, you will realize that you already know the answer, and have the technique.

Remember how stimulus-response transactions work, with an internalization in the middle? Simply recognize that there will be a number of sharp twists and small setbacks during the conflict portion of the scene, and your viewpoint character will experience each of these turns as a *stimulus*; before he replies in most cases you the author have the option of going into his brief *internalization* concerning what was just said or done. It is in these internalizations that you can remind the reader what's at stake, and how things seem to be going in the opinion of the viewpoint character.

One example of this technique has already been provided for you in the extended example from one of my own novels you read in chapter 3. At that time, it did not seem fitting to make an issue of the role of the character Collie Davis's internalizations, as we were focusing on other aspects of stimulus and response. But now you may wish to review that excerpt again.

The fact that you may also do things to further characterize the viewpoint character during such periodic brief internalizations is a bonus factor that's discussed at greater length in chapter 9.

To cast some of what's just been said in a negative way for added clarity, let's put it this way: Anytime you change viewpoint inside an ongoing scene, you risk confusing the reader about the goal, losing reader sympathy for the desired character, putting the spotlight of reader-identification in the wrong place, and muddying the dramatic waters in terms of what is at stake for whom—and even where the reader is to imagine himself "being" and experiencing what's happening.

The moral: Unless you are an accomplished, published professional with very sound tactical reasons for doing so, avoid those viewpoint changes inside a scene.

5. Disaster works (moves the story *forward*) by seeming to move the central figure *further back* from his goal, leaving him in worse trouble than he was before the scene started.

It may seem paradoxical to beginning novelists that scenes work best when they move the lead character further from his story goal—that *the best narrative progress often appears to be backwards.*

But even the simple little story of the old woman and her pig illustrates the point. As she got further and further from actually dealing directly with the pig, she seemed to be going further and further backwards. Progress in fiction is seldom two-steps-forward, then two more steps forward. Progress is often two-steps-forward, one-step-back, or even one-step-backward followed by *another* step backward.

This does not mean that your story should run backward in terms of story time. But as the hours and days of your story move ahead—and your character struggles ahead (he thinks) in trying to reach his long-term goal—he should often find himself (as the result of a scene-ending disaster) facing yet another obstacle in his path, and seeming to be in worse trouble than he ever was before.

To word this differently: Well-planned scenes end with disasters that tighten the noose around the lead character's neck; they make things *worse*, not better; they eliminate hoped-for avenues of progress; they increase the lead character's worry, sense of possible failure, and desperation—so that in all these ways the main character in a novel of 400 pages will be in *far worse shape* by page 200 than he seemed to be at the outset.

It's axiomatic among professional novelists that when things are going hideously for the lead character, the book is probably going along just wonderfully, thank you.

The following is one example of how all this works:

In *Tiebreaker*, the novel which began my series of suspense books about the character named Brad Smith, Brad begins wanting mainly to be left alone and never bothered again by his former CIA masters. But in trying to convince them that he should be left alone, he is maneuvered into accepting an assignment in Belgrade, Yugoslavia, when that country was still behind the Iron Curtain. Brad goes to Belgrade with the assignment of helping a young woman escape the country. But as a result of trying, he becomes suspected by the Yugoslavian secret police and is then "dumped" by his CIA bosses, who tell him to forget the whole thing and come home. But as a result of this action by his bosses (and scenes in which he tried to be indifferent to the young woman, but instead fell in love with her), Brad finds himself, two-thirds of the way through the novel, *not only* still doing CIA-type work, and *not only* in Yugoslavia, and *not only* trying to get the young woman out, and *not only* a suspect being watched by the dread Yugoslav secret police, and *not only* now feeling vastly conflicted by his love for the woman, and *not only* with time running out, *but also even in worse shape than all that* because he is now working absolutely alone — with both the dread UDBA and his own former masters working to thwart his effort to get the woman out. All of which has put Brad in so much more trouble than he was at the outset that now it appears *he* won't get out alive, much less rescue the young woman. He has made enormous progress — backward. (An excerpt from this novel appears in Appendix 3.)

I give you this illustration and ask you to think about it as you devise and write your own scenes. Remembering chapter 5 — that it is possible to go too far in setting up disastrous results — you should not be afraid to keep making matters worse for your hero, and you should be quite pleased with yourself if he sometimes seems to be getting into worse and worse trouble — and further and further from his goal. It is of such seemingly reverse direction that tight plot suspense and reader fascination are built.

Of course you can console yourself (but don't tell our readers!) with the secret knowledge that all of this seeming backward movement is only a dramatic illusion. As my man Brad stumbles into deeper and deeper trouble, he is in fact getting more and more desperate — learning more and more about his ghastly situation — trying various options and eliminating them as they disastrously fail — and running out of time. Metaphorically, at the start of the novel he stands at the wide end of a huge funnel of options and contingencies. But everything seems to end in disaster, scene after scene. But he plugs toward his story goal, going deeper and deeper into the funnel — his situation, his options and his time squeezing in tighter and tighter around him until there is finally only one option left — which he has to take at the climax of the book, or die.

So now you see why point 6, listed earlier, fits so closely into this discussion:

6. Readers will put up with a lot if your scenes will only keep making things worse!

The process of apparent "backward progress" in working fiction can be seen as an elimination of options that is closing the walls in on your main character, and bringing him closer all the time to the inevitable final showdown. In planning your scenes, and writing them, this general pattern of

tightening—of seeming to move backward, further from possible attainment of the story goal—should always be in your mind. Devise and write
your scenes so that each makes things worse, never better. Seldom risk a
scene ending with a disaster that only reaffirms the status quo. *Don't* fall
into the trap of writing scenes which end saying, in effect, "Well, it was 33
percent bad before, and this is terrible because it's still 33 percent bad
after this scene." Things must grow more and more gloomy, and the way
you plan your scenes, remembering the big plot picture, can assure that
this continual further darkening does take place.

The result—making matters worse and worse for the character—
will fascinate and worry your readers. They will put up with a lot of plot
tinkering and even some cumbersome writing on your part now and again
if you will keep things getting worse in this way! Remember that, and trust
the dynamic of "backward movement" to keep them enticed.

7. You can seldom, if ever plan, write or revise a scene in isolation of
your other plans for your story, because the end of each scene dictates a
lot about what can happen later.

I believe our discussion has already shown why this is so. Good scenes
have important goals and strong conflict. The conflict leads to meaningful
disaster. A meaningful disaster *changes things* so they can never be the
same again—puts the hero in worse trouble. Every scene, consequently,
must have impact on further development of your plot. You simply can't
have a "good scene" that has no later impact on events; good scenes always
have impact on later events.

Let me say this a different way, alluding to something discussed in
chapter 2. Change is threatening. Your story starts with change. But *the
disaster at the end of every scene signifies new change, which is newly threatening*.
Just as your character had to react to the change that started the story, he
must react to each change coming out of the scene-ending disaster. So he
can never be passive, your story can never become static, and every scene
must have effect sooner or later in the story—and probably sooner—because your lead character is going to react to this latest threatening
change, and try to deal with that.

This point is illustrated in the excerpt in Appendix 3. Brad Smith
opens his scene with Collie Davis by being angry with Davis's unautho-
rized entry into his condominium, and having the goal of learning what
Davis wants. By the end of the scene, Brad has a good idea of what Davis
wants from him—which is bad enough—but Brad's concluding internalization notes that Davis is also a liar . . . which hints to the reader that
this assignment will not be the piece of cake that Davis pretends. Brad is
definitely in worse trouble as a result of the action that has just taken
place. And because he is the kind of character he is, further action on his
part is obviously coming.

This dynamic, inevitable linkage between scenes in a cause and effect
pattern is one of the reasons why I suggested to you at the end of the last
chapter that you should plan some scenes, and expressed the hope that

at least some of them would link. If the scenes you planned on your cards then did not link, let me urge you to try planning more scenes which do link in a cause and effect fashion. For just as stimulus brings on response, every scene should just as inexorably bring on another scene. Once you have this structural principle well in hand, every other aspect of your writing will begin to fall into place.

TWELVE ADDITIONAL TIPS

Finally, here are some other observations that should help you plan, write and revise scenes.

    1. Make sure that the stated scene goal is clearly relevant to the story question. Don't just assume that the relevance is obvious. Spell it out.

    2. Show clearly that the viewpoint character considers the oncoming scene as vitally important. Have him say so, or think so, or both! *Never* allow a lead character to enter a scene with a lackadaisical attitude.

    3. Make sure you have provided enough background for the opposition character—or have him state enough motivation at the outset—to justify his opposition to the lead character in the scene. Don't just have someone be antagonistic on general principles!

    4. Make sure your opposing character clearly states his opposition early in the scene, and never lets up.

    5. Mentally devise a moving game plan for both the lead character and the antagonist so that even if you don't tell the reader what either is thinking, *you know what both are thinking.* This awareness of your character's thoughts, as the conflict moves along, will help you to imagine and bring out more angles—more feints and parries—in the conflict as it develops.

    6. In searching for your scene-ending disaster, don't always grab the first idea that comes to your mind. Your reader will be guessing along with you, and you don't want him to outguess you and anticipate the disaster before you give it to him. Chances are that if you make a list of six or eight possible disasters that would work, one of them well down the list from your first idea will be fresher, brighter, worse for the lead character—and not predictable by the reader. You always want the reader kept guessing!

    7. Don't be afraid to have your antagonist try to get the lead character "off the point" of argument as one of his opposing tactics. Just make sure that your lead character keeps reiterating his scene goal—and fighting to keep the argument on the central subject.

    8. Don't hesitate to use *dialogue at cross-purposes* once in a while as a scene-building device. Such dialogue can be defined as story conversation in which the conflict is not overt, but where the antagonist either doesn't understand what's really at issue, or is purposely nonresponsive to what the lead character keeps trying to talk about. Dialogue at cross-purposes, or nonresponsive behavior by an antagonist, will be experienced by both the lead character *and* the reader as conflictual. After all, in such a situa-

tion the lead character feels thwarted in some way, and so struggles harder. If the opposing character does not start responding quite directly, the viewpoint character will fight harder.

(Again, the excerpt in Appendix 3 illustrates the point.)

One caveat, however: The use of this dialogue device cannot substitute for genuine conflict over the length of many chapters. It is for *occasional* use only, when information must be transmitted to the reader through a story conversation, and the author wants to avoid the dullness of one character simply lecturing the other about facts the reader needs to be told.

9. Remember, in building conflict in the scene and in devising your disaster, that people are not always entirely rational, especially in stress situations. If your antagonist loses his temper and says or does something that would be crazy in other circumstances, maybe it's okay. Think about his character as you've built it, and if his craziness seems "in character," given this stressful conflict segment, then consider allowing him to blow up or make some stupid mistake. Your story people — even in the toughest scenes — are not wholly logical robots.

10. Plan and write the scene for all you can get out of it. Revise if its impact suddenly seems too great for what your plot calls for next, and cut it only if you reread it later and sense that it may get dull in spots — or if the overall pacing of your novel requires that this particular segment be boiled to hurry general story progress along.

11. Always be alert for ways to raise the stakes in a scene, as long as you don't turn it into Armageddon.

12. Never let your characters relax or feel comfortable in a scene.

Having given all this your best thought and effort, I hope you will be far along toward understanding how scenes are built, and how they form the essential action component in the structure of a novel. I hope, too, you see how they themselves are structured internally — and how they move a story along with the same narrative force that makes response follow stimulus . . . effect follow cause. As writers we come to understand more about how fiction works; it's delightful to begin to understand how structural principles are the same from line to line to scene to scene to chapter to chapter — how the governing law in all cases is that of cause and effect.

In the next chapter we'll start considering how to connect scenes, and how better to motivate them.

Oh, and in case you were wondering about the old woman and the pig, the climax came — much later — in a sequence something like this:

The maid began to scold the cat, the cat began to kill the rat, the rat began to gnaw the rope, the rope began to hang the butcher, the butcher began to kill the cow, the cow began to drink the water, the water began to quench the fire, the fire began to burn the stick, the stick began to beat the dog, the dog began to bite the pig, the pig jumped over the stile — and the old woman got home that night!

As we'll see later, especially in chapters 11 and 12, plotting your novel with scenes will not result in a climax involving this kind of domino effect tumbling in reverse through the story's earlier causations. We've gotten a bit more sophisticated than that. But this ending was just fine for that two year old I was so long ago.

CHAPTER 7

LINKING YOUR SCENES: THE STRUCTURE OF SEQUEL

IF YOU'VE BEEN FOLLOWING ALONG through the discussion of scene structure, with all its implications for linkage of such scenes, each leading to the next in cause-and-effect fashion, you have surely begun to see how a tight, logical, suspenseful plot can be built from scenes in a manner that provides continual surprises for the reader. But there was one major problem you might also have noticed: the requirement that the scene be told moment by moment to be as lifelike and reader-involving as possible.

"Wait a minute!" you may have thought. "If I try to tell every bit of my story in scenes—and each is told moment by moment—then the story of a single day could turn out to be longer than *War and Peace*."

And it may have also occurred to you that the moments of internalization that might take place during the stimulus-response transactions that make up a scene provide precious little time for the viewpoint character to think or feel—and little space for the author to write them down for the purposes of characterization of analysis of character motivation.

Clearly, in any long story there must be some structural component besides the scene.

There are essentially two: *transition* and *sequel*.

Transition is a very simple device which provides a direct statement to the reader to the effect that a change in time, place or viewpoint has happened since the last scene. Such transitions can be as simple as the following:

> It was the following Tuesday when they met again. *Or,*
> At about the same time Joe met Bill, another meeting was taking place on the other side of town. *Or,*
> Three hours later . . . *Or,*
> In another office far from Gotham City . . . *Or even,*
> Meanwhile, back at the ranch . . . !

Such simple transitions sometimes are enough to serve as the bridge to carry your reader from one scene to another. But clearly, if you want to deal in any depth with a character's emotional state, or show his thought processes as he analyzes his plight and makes future plans, or use his thinking process to give the reader information about things that happened before the story started (or in the time that has elapsed between chapters), then you need something bigger and better than a simple transition.

That "something"—the sequel—is the glue that holds scenes together and helps you get from one to the next. It is a flexible structural component, and it provides you with all the tools you need for in-depth characterization, analysis of motivation, explanation of character planning, etc.

In an ideal Platonic world, there would be a sequel between every pair of scenes. Often you will see modern novels in which scene causes sequel which leads into next scene, which causes next sequel, and so on. Indeed, most novelists plan their stories in just this scene-sequel, scene-sequel pattern. But because they are so flexible in length and content requirements, sequels are often much harder to spot in finished fiction.

This, however, does not mean that they do not have a prototypical, ideal internal structure. They definitely do.

A NEW START

A sequel begins for your viewpoint character the moment a scene ends. Just struck by a new, unanticipated but logical disaster, he is plunged into a period of sheer *emotion*, followed sooner or later by a period of *thought*, which sooner or later results in the formation of a new, goal-oriented *decision*, which in turn results in some *action* toward the new goal just selected.

And what do you have when the decision made in the sequel's decision segment is turned into some new, goal-oriented action? Add another character who will oppose the new action, and you have conflict—you are into the next scene.

If you pause to think a moment about how people really react to disaster in their actual lives, you will see that the first reaction to such a setback is emotional. "My God!" Bill cries, and hits the palm of his hand to his forehead. Or, "How can that *be*?" Jean demands, tears filling her eyes. Or, momentarily crushed by his setback, David slumps to the floor in speechless, wide-eyed shock.

We best see emotion as the first stage of reaction to disaster when we witness someone's loss of a loved one. Very often the emotional reaction is so intense that the bereaved person loses almost all control, dissolving in tears or becoming hysterical, sometimes requiring sedation. The length of time the purely emotional reaction retains domination of the person depends on the kind of person he or she is, the nature and depth of the shock, and perhaps other circumstances as well.

However long the period of pure emotional reaction is, however, just about every normal person will get through it at some point and start thinking again. This transition to thought may be quick or it may be marked by numerous relapses into pure emotion again. However it comes, though, rational process starts percolating again. The person has moved from *emotion* into *thought*.

Thus the first two stages of sequel in fiction closely parallel what actually happens to us after a real-life disaster. In real life, there are tragic figures who never get beyond this thought stage, brooding the rest of their lives about their setback or loss. But in fiction we need movement *forward*, and so we look to the pattern followed by people who have gotten beyond a disaster to see how their process went on.

When we do this, we see that people who move beyond disaster will slowly focus their thoughts on some new *decision* that they hope will make things better. And, having made this decision, if it is to have meaning, at some point they *act upon it.*

So, because we want forward movement in our fiction—and decided at the outset to write about people with the courage and the will to take their own lives by the scruff of the neck and *make things better*, we structure our fiction sequels with decision and new action.

Emotion . . . thought . . . decision . . . action. The four structural compartments of the sequel. Sequels thus get a character from one disaster to the start of the next scene.

Now, because it often delves deeply into the head and heart of a viewpoint character, sequel is not "stage-able" like the scene. Sequel is often wholly internal. And because it focuses on often-painful reactions which might pass in a moment—but could also require hours, days or even weeks to get through—sequel cannot be told moment by moment, as in a scene. In sequel, you can and probably must have summary. In sequel, you can show a character alone, and dig deep into his thoughts and feelings. In sequel, you seek feeling and understanding by the reader—*sympathy*.

Thus, while a scene is characterized by conflict, which is exciting and told moment by moment, a sequel is characterized by feeling and logic, and can span great chunks of time or space. (Occasionally, as mentioned earlier, you may get by with simply summarizing some plot action or using a simple "Later, downtown . . ." transitional sentence or paragraph. But here we are looking at a *developed* story component—one which delves deeply into the character's reactions to what has just happened to him.)

There is another striking difference between scene and sequel which illustrates the potential flexibility of sequel. As we have learned, the goal portion of a scene usually takes only a few lines at most, and the disaster often is shown in even less space; virtually all of the interior structure of a scene is devoted to conflict—and this is an unvarying structural rule. But in the sequel, how much space you devote to each structural component is entirely flexible, depending on your impulses as a writer, the kind of story you may be writing at the moment, the kind of viewpoint character you are dealing with, the harshness of the disaster that has just happened, the complexity of factors the character must consider in trying to reach a new decision, and even some other factors that will become apparent only in chapter 8. Little about sequel structure is hard-and-fast, except that the *sequence* of the parts must always be imagined by the writer in the order which human behavior dictates—emotion first, then later thought, then the reaching of a decision, then a new, goal-oriented action.

Let's consider each part of the prototypical sequel in a bit more detail.

Emotion

Reeling back in the aftermath of a scene-ending disaster, your character first experiences mixed feelings that may be quite chaotic: anger mixed with surprise, fear mixed with resentment, bitterness mixed with disappointment and suspicion, and so on. In this first portion of a full-blown sequel, you are dealing with the problem of portraying a person who is not yet quite rational as a result of what has just happened. Portraying such an emotional state in a character is often very difficult, but in some types of books such as the contemporary romance it must be done in considerable depth.

How do you present such an emotional segment? You use every bit of imagination you possess, and place yourself in the heart and head of your suffering character. Knowing everything you know about what has happened earlier in the story, the importance of the scene goal that has just been denied, the strength of your character's motivation, the importance of the long-term story goal, and the depth of your character's surprise, you imagine not merely what *you* might feel in such a situation, but what *this character* must be feeling. Then you devise ways to show and tell this strong emotional state.

Essentially there are three ways to give this emotional state to your reader. You can do it by description, by example, or by discussion.

Description

Description of emotion means just what it says. You sit at your keyboard and do your best to describe the character's internal emotions. Often such description is virtually timeless: time seems to stand still as you describe the pain or rage or whatever feelings are there. Some writers can beautifully describe emotion in a character, while others find it one of the hardest jobs in fiction.

Example

When you choose instead to get the emotion across to your reader by example, you search for gestures or actions the character might take which would show the reader the results of the inner storm. For anger, you might show your hero slamming his fist through a thin office partition, for example, or hurling a telephone. For sadness, you might show him dabbing at wet eyes, blowing his nose, then crumpling into his chair to stare like a zombie. For confusion, you might show him striking his own forehead with his hand, walking aimlessly, forgetting an important appointment, failing to follow a conversation. Any combination of actions may be devised to illustrate to the reader that strong emotion is raging beneath this surface.

While use of example is not as direct, obviously, as description, and does run some small risk of reader misunderstanding, it has the advantage of allowing the reader to observe, then *reach his own conclusion*. This is how we often recognize strong emotion in real life, and so it's convincing if you the author choose the right behavioral signals. In addition, a reader who intuits character feeling from observation of examples can be counted on to make a leap in his own imagination, and vicariously experience similar feelings based on some experience in his own actual past life. This kind of reader leap of identification and sympathy may actually turn out to be stronger than any emotion you might be able to arouse in him by torturous direct description.

Discussion

And what about it? Here we use an entirely different technique and stop being inside the character to any great extent, or with the character in isolation. Rather than trying to provide a static description of how the character is feeling, or showing him doing things that will help the reader intuit those feelings, in *discussion* we set up a situation where our character talks to someone else — a friend, a lover, perhaps even a doctor — and has a conversation with the other person about how he is feeling.

Your reader in this case watches what appears to be a scene unfolding: two people talking. And in a way the resultant story component almost is a scene in its external trappings — dialogue, movement, gestures, etc. — but the *intent* is to allow the character to speak of his emotions, be questioned about them by the other person, and perhaps even experience new emotions as a result of feeling misunderstood, or something of that nature.

How will you present the emotional part of a sequel? Probably by using each of these techniques as seems appropriate at the time, and sometimes by mixing them together — a description section, for example, interrupted by the entry of a friend who says, "You look like you feel terrible! Tell me about it!"

And *how long* will the emotional section be? Again: This will depend in very large measure on your intentions as a writer, the kind of story, the kind of character, and so on. In a modern romance novel, the emotional compartment may be described for page after page. In a chilly suspense novel, it may be slashed to a few words. Your "feel" for your character and situation will help you decide, and things you'll learn in the next handful of pages will help you, too.

The first excerpt in Appendix 4, as brief as it is, illustrates one way to hint at emotion without directly describing it. The female character looks back on a meeting with a fascinating man and remembers little of the factual content of their conversation. The reader senses how emotionally overwrought the woman must have been — how intensely she felt then, *and feels now*, without the author's use of lengthy description or analysis of any kind.

Thought

For now, let's move on by noting that at some point your character will move out of blind feeling and into *thought*. At first this thought may be somewhat haphazard and confused by emotion. But sooner or later (again, depending on the kind of character, story, etc.), he will begin thinking rationally.

As he does this, his process will usually break down into the following structural pattern:

Review

In which he looks back on the scene that just played, remembers the disaster and what it means in terms of his hopes, thinks again about his story goal and why it's important, and thinks back to other aspects of the earlier story that may be determined in part by the kind of story it is. (In a mystery, the detective might here review earlier clues; in a romance, the heroine might recall earlier dates with her lover.)

This process of review may (again) be very brief sometimes, very long and involved others, depending on story situation. It can serve as a wonderful tool for you the author in the midst of writing a novel, because as the character reviews, he is reminding the reader what has happened and why it's important.

Analysis

After reviewing, the character ordinarily moves into analysis, a short or longer period of thought in which he tries to figure out the meaning of everything that has happened, especially the most recent disaster. Again, this analytical thought process can be used by you the author to remind the reader of what's important — or possibly to make sure the reader understands some things about the plot. As the character analyzes, he also tends to further characterize himself as well, because how he analyzes will show more about how he thinks — what kind of person he is.

Planning

Out of analysis comes planning. Here, taking into account all the factors he can think of, your character tries to lay out a new plan so that he can struggle forward toward his story goal. He considers options, weighs them, discards some, rank-orders the rest. It is here that you as the author-in-charge show your character taking hold of the story and in effect laying out the next steps in the plot for the reader.

In my own writing, I usually have a very clear idea of where I want the story to go next, and what I want to happen as a result. But I constantly remind myself that I cannot simply "push the characters" into what I as author want next; instead, I have to sit back from the keyboard during the thought section of the sequel, review *my* author desires and intentions for future developments in the plot, then put myself imaginatively into my viewpoint character's head and search for emotional and logical reasons why he or she would arrive at the same decision for next action that I the author want.

In one of my recent novels published under a pseudonym which I don't want to reveal, my heroine at one crucial turning point *must* decide to visit the room of a sick person in the retirement center where the heroine works. She has just learned at the end of a scene that the resident is more ill than she had imagined; but there are both a doctor and a nurse on duty, and there seemed to me at first to be no emotional or logical reason for my very-busy heroine to drop everything and fall even further behind in her pressing work to pay a visit when such good care is already available. But that was exactly what my plot plans required that she somehow logically do.

It took considerable doing on my part to have my heroine feel terribly shocked to learn how serious the illness might be . . . then review her fine relationship with the sick person . . . then realize that good care was being provided . . . but then decide that she would never be able to work efficiently this day as long as she remained so worried and preoccupied, and that *she owed it to herself*—to make herself feel more at ease about the illness—to make a brief visit to the sick person's room and reassure herself that the sick friend did not appear at death's door. Only in this way, she decided, would she have enough peace of mind to return to her overloaded work schedule and try to get caught up.

In this way I was able to build logic into a key turning point of the story and make my heroine's immediate cessation of regular work, and visit to the sick room, believable. But none of this would have been possible if I hadn't put myself into my character's feelings and thoughts.

Decision

In the above example, we have already leaped ahead into decision, so tightly woven are sequel components. The decision comes after your character has gone through as many steps as you find necessary in the process of reviewing, analyzing and planning. The decision to be made is not a generality, but a specific new, short-term, goal-oriented one. He sees now, despite all the bad things that have happened, some new ray of hope— some new gambit he can try, suspect he can question, search he can make, request he can lodge. He considers it from all angles and sees that it is his best hope to reenter the fray and again fight toward his story goal.

This is not always necessarily a simple thing. Even after picking his goal, the character may have to brood about ways to try to achieve it. "Snap judgments" are seldom convincing as sequel decisions. The character may still be nagged by doubts, worried, scared, and confused. But he finally decides on something—the best course of action he can imagine at the moment. *Almost always, you the author make this new goal crystal clear.*

Why should you be careful to make the newly selected goal clear? For at least three reasons. First, it's important for the reader to realize that the character has picked a new course of action and is ready to move into it; seeing that a specific new goal has been selected not only proves that the sequel has been important, and will now change the future course of the story; it also clarifies the logical linkage between what has gone before and what is to come next. Second, stipulation of the new goal begins to prepare the reader for the next confrontation or scene; it heightens anticipation and suspense. Third, we have already seen that understanding of the scene goal is vital to the reader's understanding of the scene and the things that are at stake; mentioning the scene goal late in the sequel preceding it adds to potential clarity about the scene goal and its potential consequences when the character later enters the scene, states the goal once more, and reenters the fray.

Action

In the conclusion of his sequel, your character gets back into movement again — new action — making an appointment, a telephone call, buying an airplane ticket, or doing whatever it takes to start him on his way to the time and place where he stands facing some new person. He states (again) his just-reached goal — and is plunged into another scene.

The second excerpt in Appendix 4 illustrates many of the points we have been discussing. Having just experienced a major disaster (in this case a fall down an abandoned mine shaft), the viewpoint character experiences almost-paralyzing emotion, then thinks about her plight, finally makes a difficult decision, and takes the first step toward a new series of actions.

Thus sequel links your scenes by showing how your character gets from one to the next both psychologically and physically. If you think about it, you will see how sequel is an enormously expanded internalization — so that the dynamic of something happening *outside* results in something happening *inside*, whichever structural level you happen to be at. In the microcosm, stimulus leads to internalization which leads to response by cause and effect. In the macrocosm, scene leads to sequel which leads to another scene by the same process.

How long will your sequels be? Obviously, since many factors may influence how long you make any given part of a sequel, the length of sequels varies enormously.

Just as some writers tend naturally to write rather lengthy internalizations during their stimulus-response transactions, some writers will tend to dwell on sequel, even sometimes skipping a scene to then write an enormously detailed sequel in which the content of the skipped scene can be condensed . . . analyzed . . . interpreted . . . or even misunderstood by the viewpoint character thinking about what took place in the story *but was not shown to the reader* because the scene was skipped.

Some novelists, for example, are more interested in their characters' reactions to events than in the events themselves. We can find great chunks of a novel composed almost entirely of *sequels to scenes that were skipped over*. Such a general structure requires the novelist to plan the story in the conventional scene-sequel sequence, then figure out ways to not write many of the scenes, yet present a condensed, interpreted version of what was in those scenes during a subsequent sequel.

This is a highly complex and specialized technique, and I don't recommend it. For the writer capable of handling it, however, it provides some advantages. For one thing, parts of planned scenes that might be tedious to even a small degree can be condensed or left out if they are recounted in the structure of sequel-recollection, because the sequel form does allow condensation. Also, putting your story mainly in sequel form allows somewhat deeper characterization because so much more of the story is seen through a more subjective lens—a character's *interpretation* becoming an integral part of every event. Finally, the nature of sequel allows for a slower, more thoughtful pace—about which more will be said in the chapter that follows this one.

To summarize this point, sequels may be very, very long indeed, and in a specialized technique may not only link scenes logically and emotionally, but virtually replace many scenes by reviewing them after the fact.

But the important point for you the author to remember is this: Even when the final structure of a novel so emphasizes sequel, and downplays scenes, *the author had to plan all the story in classic scene-sequel sequence* to be able to present it in this unusual fashion.

You must always plan the normal, fully developed scene-sequel sequence, however you may end up presenting the material to your reader.

Just as some writers tend to write very long sequels, more tend to write short ones. Further, just as it was not always necessary to "play" the internalization of a stimulus-response transaction for your reader when the transaction was very simple and straightforward, you may find that there are times in the actual writing of your story when the character's emotional response is so obvious, and his next course of action so clearcut and immediately required, that you either do no more than hint at a sequel in a sentence or two—and get right on with the next scene—or possibly even cut a possible sequel entirely.

Let's consider each of these options.

SEQUEL VARIATIONS

Given a scene-ending disaster which demands *immediate* new responsive action by the viewpoint character, you may write a sequel that collapses all the classic sequel elements into the briefest wordage, something like this:

> As she saw Brad slump back in the pilot's seat and the Cessna start to roll, (*Emotion*) Connie froze with terror. (*Thought component skipped.*) (*Decision*) All she could do was try to take over. (*Action*) She grasped the control yoke and . . .

And Connie is into the next scene — in this case fighting the aircraft as if it were a live antagonist, her goal being to get it under control and safely down.

Sometimes the pressure is even graver, and scenes must simply collide because insertion of a linking sequel is not only unnecessary but would appear absurd if you tried to stop the story action long enough to put one in.

Suppose, for example, that your scene-ending disaster was a "*Yes, but!*" development: Your hero stubbornly questioned the suspect in the suspect's apartment, his goal being to get the suspect to admit he owned a .45 automatic. At the end of the scene, the disaster is as follows:

> Simpson walked to the desk and opened a drawer. "All right," he said, face contorted by rage. "You want to know if I own a gun like the murder weapon? Yes."
> As he spoke, Simpson took a .45 automatic out of the drawer and aimed it at Hero's head.
> "I'm sorry," Simpson said, thumbing the hammer of the weapon back. "But now you have to die."
> Hero saw Simpson's hand start to tighten on the trigger.

Given a disaster of this magnitude, obviously demanding such an immediate response, our hero better not be allowed to try to start having a classically developed sequel. If he does, he's a dead man. He has to act, and the range of his options is not very great: duck, jump, roll, yell something (though the good Lord only knows what that might be!) — or die.

This kind of pressure of time is the greatest killer of sequels known to man. Even if your hero is presented with a much more complex situation, with many more possible options, none of which looks very good, time pressure may force him to do something *right now*. Faced with entrapment in a burning building or a child's plunge through thin ice into the freezing lake, for example, your character *might* have all sorts of terrible emotional reactions and complex thoughts *if there were time*. But since there is no time, he has to act at once, without the luxury of sorting through his feelings or considering possible alternative actions. In the burning building, he has to get out, possibly trying to rescue someone with him. Faced with the child screaming from the hole in the ice, he has to throw a rope, jump in himself, run for help or whatever. But in no case does time allow much thinking about it.

Thus you will find that some scene-ending disasters are of a nature that make sequel unnecessary or impossible. But it's a funny thing about most fiction readers: They understand scene-sequel structure so well *at a subconscious level*, having read it all their lives, that they expect sequel to follow scene, and like it if you can provide some aspect of sequel to a given disaster — even one demanding immediate action. It's as if the reader unconsciously knows that a sequel should "play" immediately after the father sees his child fall through the ice; the reader also knows there is no time for a sequel then and there. But *later there may be some time*. And that's when the wise fiction writer will allow the viewpoint character to recall, or talk about, how he felt and what he thought in a flash at the moment after the disaster.

You'll see the hero somehow manage to save the child. You'll see a trip to the hospital, a talk with doctors, all manner of action, perhaps, immediately following the fall through the ice. But, at some point later in the narrative, the wise writer will often go back to the moment of possible sequel *and tell about it after the fact* to satisfy the reader's innate sense of form and yearning for completion of pattern.

Something like this:

> It was midnight, ten hours after the incident. Sitting in front of the fireplace, Madison sipped his brandy and shuddered violently. "When I saw Jimmy fall through the ice," he said slowly, "it was as if someone had hit me in the chest with a sledgehammer. I've never experienced such sheer horror. I knew I didn't have time to think, but in a single instant it was as if . . ." (etc., etc.)

Is there a moral here for you when you are planning and writing your sequence of scenes and sequels? I think so, and it's simply this: Anytime you skip a sequel, however good the reason, you should ask yourself if you need to tell something about that sequel later in the story—when there is more time, perhaps—to satisfy your reader's need for structural completion of a scene-sequel cycle.

Sometimes your answer will be "yes," and you will devise a quiet moment in the story in which your hero can ruminate, inwardly or aloud to another character. Such reviews by a character out of the normal order of things can be effective devices to intensify reader understanding and sympathy.

Other times you will decide that the time pressure which forced omission of the sequel in its natural sequence was so obvious—and his resulting action so inevitable—that no later rumination is necessary. If you make this decision, then of course you need not create a moment later in the story to allow such reflection. Which course you take depends on the factors already mentioned, and others, such as how well the reader already knows the character from earlier portions of the story, how intense the time pressure on your character continues to be, and how you want to control the general pace of the tale. (More about some of these factors in chapter 8.)

As a working assignment to clarify your thinking about sequels and how they work, let me suggest that you take the scene cards with which you worked earlier, designing scenes and then working to find some which would logically link. Now design sequels which would fit between these scenes, linking them more closely. Identify each compartment of the sequel, and write at least a sentence or two describing that emotion, that thought segment, that decision, that new action.

Having done this work, look at some of your previous writing and see how well you have practiced classic sequel structure in the past. See if you might improve any transitional passages now that you understand so much more about sequel structure. Even if the pages you revise do not happen to be part of a manuscript you consider potentially salable, the work will pay dividends in engraining better work habits and making the structure of both scene and sequel ever more clear as you actually create within the boundaries of the structures.

Another exercise which my students have found most helpful over the years is to select a published popular novel, preferably one of your favorites, and mark up a few chapters for scene and sequel—and also the component parts of each scene and sequel. (I personally detest marking in my books, but this work is so potentially helpful that I make the suggestion anyway.)

If you do this marking, you will find variations in structure of the kinds we have already discussed, and perhaps some that are yet to be described in this book. The analysis—again—will help you not only by showing you classic structure, but those interesting variations as well.

Always—when you find a variation, study it carefully and ask yourself why the writer handled the structure as she did. Make notes in your workbook, your journal, or elsewhere—questions yet to be answered, observations about techniques that will be of use to you, or whatever.

In addition, you may wish to devise a series of imagined story disasters with an obvious and predictable emotional reaction and final decision—then work to plan out a sequel in all its steps which would move the character *through reactions and thoughts unlikely to be anticipated by the reader, and to some decision that is not the obvious one—one the reader would not easily predict.*

The second excerpt in Appendix 4 provides an example of such a sequel. It was vital to me as the author to get my heroine away from the place where she fell. The most obvious thing for most people to do, however, would be to sit tight and wait, hoping to be rescued. As you study the excerpt, notice how the heroine's feelings and thoughts are subtly moved along to bring her to the author-desired decision and new action—movement.

For your exercise, consider some of the following disasters which would tend to have a predictable sequel pattern and resulting new decision. Then devise different sequel patterns that would logically lead to quite a different new decision.

Here are some sample "workbook disasters":

1. A man very much in love with his wife learns that she is having a long-term, passionate affair. (Instead of being hurt or outraged, and confronting her or her lover, can you devise reactions and thoughts which would instead convince him to feel *relief*—and decide to buy her a nice present while saying nothing?)

2. An executive of a large manufacturing firm is notified that her plant has just burned to the ground. (Instead of shock or dismay, and plans to rebuild, can you devise a sequel in which she would feel only a remote sadness—and decide to go on an ocean cruise?)

3. A young woman is told she has won a coveted scholarship to medical school. (Instead of pleasure and new plans to move to the school, can you devise a sequel that would have her burst into tears and logically decide to take a job in the local factory instead?)

It would be cheating you of the work to suggest possible solutions to these example problems. Besides, you may wish to devise your own list, and work through those.

Only after study of the excerpts and work on sequel planning of your own will you be ready to move on to the next chapter of this book.

See Appendix 4.

CHAPTER 8

SCENE-SEQUEL TRICKS TO CONTROL PACE

ONCE UPON A TIME there was a very young, unpublished writer (who shall be nameless, except that his initials were J.M.B.) who decided after having written several unsold novels that he would write the wildest, fastest-moving, slam-bang adventure he could think of. He made a list of exciting, stirring events, and wrote the novel from the list. To his great astonishment and greater chagrin, the novel turned out slow-moving, pseudo-thoughtful, and generally dull and insipid.

At the time he was thoroughly baffled. It was not until some years later—having had scene structure drilled into his head by professional writing coach Dwight V. Swain—that he was able to understand what had happened: He had written most of his "action book" with very long sequels and very short scenes. It was a valuable, if painful, lesson.

And the moral of this reminiscence? What did I actually learn?

If you have been drawing some of your own inferences while you study along in this book, you may be smiling because you already see what it took me so long to understand.

Scenes are exciting, conflictful, densely packed with action and dialogue, and therefore *fast-reading*.

Sequels, on the other hand, are thoughtful, can be extended, have summary in them, and are therefore *slow-reading*.

To put this another way, the scene portions of your book seem to the reader to go very fast. The sequels seem to go much slower.

What does this imply for you as a novelist? Simply this: You can control the pace of your novel at every turn by how you handle your scenes and sequels. If it seems to be going too slowly, you need to build your scenes and possibly trim or cut out some of your sequels. On the other hand, if it seems to be going too fast, you need to do the opposite: Trim or cut some of your scenes, and build up your sequels.

TECHNIQUES TO SPEED THE STORY ALONG

Suppose the story seems to be going too slowly. Here, more specifically, are some of the things you can do to speed things up:

1. In those places where you find a developed sequel linking two scenes that follow one another in a fairly straightforward and logical way, consider yanking the sequel entirely and simply butting the two scenes back-to-front. If the goal and opening of conflict in the second of the two scenes seem to grow logically out of the previous disaster, your reader is not likely to be confused — and you may need speed here more than logical explanation to the *n*th degree.

2. Look for places where you might not be able to simply butt scenes end to end, but where a very simple transitional statement might get the job done. There's nothing swifter-moving than the brief transitional statement such as *"Three hours later . . ."* or *"In New York, at the Plaza . . ."*. If you find such spots, and they are presently occupied by even a truncated or abbreviated sequel, jerk out the sequel material and substitute the simple, lightning-fast transition.

3. Study your sequels with an eye toward trimming out some of the present verbiage. Ask yourself questions like "Does *all* this emotion have to be described?" and "Does he really have to review *all* of these story events at this time?

(Sometimes, of course, you will ask yourself these questions and decide that yes, every word about the emotion is necessary here, or yes, because this plot has gotten so complex, the character *must* think about everything that's happened to avoid losing the reader. If so, fine! I'm asking you to *consider* such trims or boils; I'm not ordering them.)

4. Look for places where you might have inadvertently skipped a chance to write in a big, exciting, extended scene. Analyze the dramatic potential of every confrontation between major characters, and ask yourself if you have possibly missed a chance to motivate them to struggle over some story issue at this point. Is it possible to invent some reason for one or both of the characters to enter this meeting with a stronger, more pressing immediate goal? Can you extend and intensify whatever argument already exists by raising the stakes or making the participants more desperate as a result of a preceding sequel? Have you (God forbid!) overlooked a chance to include some major confrontation that your plot has already set up as possible or even likely?

If you find such slips, by all means write the scene now and slip it into the story.

5. Examine all your present scenes and ask yourself if you can find ways to raise the stakes, increase the intensity of the conflict, add to the viewpoint character's sense of desperation, or add some secondary issues, heretofore overlooked, that the adversaries could also fight about here.

6. Consider the nature of your scene-ending disasters. Have you inadvertently made any of them less disastrous and upsetting than they might still logically be?

7. Look at the timing behind the disasters you have chosen. Have you perhaps set up a disaster so that the hero has a week or ten days to react, when it might be possible to change the disaster only marginally and make it one which requires a sequel and new action *right away*?

8. Consider the thinking of both the hero and the villain-figure in

every scene, and in general. How might you change their assumptions and plans in such a way as to tighten the time frame of the entire story, forcing scenes to come one after another much more swiftly?

Now, it's all fine and wonderful for me to give you such a list of alternatives designed to speed things up; I don't have to do it in *your* story, right? "Easy for you to talk!" you may think. But believe me, questions like those above go through my mind any number of times during the writing of one of my novels. Pacing is something that worries most novelists constantly. And the questions do not just preoccupy me during the writing. During revision, when I'm trying my hardest to stand back a little and perceive the general pacing of the entire story, such questions are again uppermost in my mind.

But perhaps your problem is just the opposite. Perhaps you've written a manuscript that seems far *too* fast: Events gallop in on the tail of other events; story people don't ever seem to find time to think; things happen so fast and furious that it almost gets ludicrous at times; it's exciting and fast, but a lot of it doesn't seem to make much sense.

In these cases, you have to slow things down. How?

Occasionally you may be able to find a scene that can be eliminated entirely, its action revealed in a later sequel. Far more often, however, you must search for scenes that you might trim or soften to shorten them. At the same time, you must search for sequels you might have failed to write in at all—and now consider supplying them; you should also study the sequels which do presently exist in your manuscript, and think about ways to expand their content and make them longer.

The list of things you do to accomplish these ends reads almost like the mirror image of the "speed-up list" just offered. But before we get to a specific list of recommendations, perhaps a word of explanation is in order. For, if I earlier sold you on the requirement that scenes be told moment by moment, with no summary and nothing left out in terms of steps in the conflict, you may very well be muttering a protest right now when you read about "trimming" a scene. "How can that be possible," I can almost hear a voice demanding, "when you can't summarize and you're supposed to follow the action moment by moment in stimulus-response fashion?"

Patience! The answer lies *not* in violating these rules, but in figuring out ways around them. By the time you finish the chapter, things will be a lot clearer.

So let's look at all your alternatives if the story is going too swiftly and recklessly.

HOW TO SLOW THINGS DOWN

1. Look for scenes that you might possibly cut entirely, telling about it in a sequel.

This is a most dangerous technique, one possible result (if you go an inch too far) being a total flattening of the story's appeal in terms of onstage action. But you might find a few scenes in a novel-length manuscript which could be cut out in this way. Such scenes will be the ones that you developed out of relatively minor, low-pressure character goals, which inevitably resulted in relatively milder conflict. These scenes are your candidates for possible elimination.

It may seem paradoxical, on first glance, to look for *weak* scenes to cut when seeking to slow your manuscript's pace. Wouldn't it be more to the point, you might legitimately ask, to slash a few really big, exciting scenes and *really* slow things down?

If you pause and think about it, you'll realize that the really big scenes are the heart and soul of your story. Cutting them out would constitute overkill — or perhaps it would be more accurate to say "professional suicide." Cut out major scenes at your own peril! Not only will the reader feel cheated, but trying to explain *everything* about a killed major scene in a later sequel may be beyond your capabilities.

Further, cutting out any scene will slow the pace. However low the intensity, *any* scene reads fast. So if you find a handful of relatively mild ones for elimination, you will accomplish almost as much in terms of slowing the pace as you would have by cutting out one that seems much bigger. It's the very structure of scene that makes it seem too fast, not just its content.

2. Look for scenes in which you might reduce the amount of story time set up for playing out the conflict.

Suppose, for example, that you set up a scene wherein your hero confronts the company board of directors, and you have the scene written now so that the hero enters the boardroom just as the meeting is getting under way — then fights the good fight for the entire day before meeting his disaster at 6 P.M. Is there any way you could change your scene assumptions so that hero is scheduled to appear before the board at 3 P.M., with only thirty minutes set aside for him on the agenda? Obviously, if he's in the scene a much shorter period of story time, the fight can't go on as long — and the number of pages you devote to it must shrink proportionately.

3. Look for scenes in which you can get the job done in terms of presenting the conflict by entering the scene *in the middle of things*.

How would this work? In the first place, you might make the character's scene goal crystal-clear in the sequel preceding it. You might then take your scene that is presently written in ten pages, covering from, say, 7 to 9 P.M., and slash you actual written presentation of the entire scene to a fragment that will get the job done dramatically. If the present scene covers two hours, ten pages, and six steps or maneuvers in the conflict, you might jump in with your presentation starting ninety minutes into the total time, with four of the six steps skipped over, something like this:

> By 8:30, John was already exhausted.
>
> "Look," he told Pettibone. "We've covered four of the six points at issue, here, but now we're down to the nitty-gritty. Let's talk about the bonus clause. . . ."

Et cetera.

It will probably hurt your artistic soul to trim out some of the earlier great conflict by jumping in in the middle this way. It always does mine. But if your pacing problem is severe enough, you may have no choice. You're working to *reduce the disproportionate predominance of scene over sequel* here, remember; you're fighting to slow down your book any way you can, and sometimes desperate measures are the only answer.

4. Consider giving your viewpoint character more internalizations during the scenes. Internalizations can't be excessively long, but if you're really having trouble slowing the pace, there's no reason why you can't occasionally make story time stand still while you show the character thinking about a lot of things in an internalization, even remembering story background theretofore not given the reader.

Such extended internalizations take place in a flash, in terms of story time, but may fill several pages of exposition *that will slow the pace for the reader*.

5. Look for ways to build in more breathing time for your viewpoint character between scenes. The main way you do this: by changing some of your scene goals or disasters so that your character will have more time for sequel before he is forced by story circumstances to act again—and go into another scene. This is precisely the opposite of what you were advised to do if you wanted to speed things up. There you altered the viewpoint character's entering goal or story situation so that a disaster in this scene would require immediate action; or you changed the nature of the disaster slightly to allow no time for a sequel to take place. Conversely, when trying to slow the story down, you set up scene goals whose thwarting will not require instant new action, or you alter the disaster so that its full impact— or new action it will require—does not have to take place at once. Gone will be some of those falling-through-the-ice disasters, and in their place will go disasters such as the child cracking the ice and *almost* falling through, so that the viewpoint character can take the child back home and then think slowly and carefully about how he should proceed to (a) convince the child not to take such risks; (b) provide more constant watching over the child, or (c) making the pond totally off-limits by building a fence around it, or some such.

6. Study your existing sequels and consider expanding one or more parts of them. Did you, for example, gloss over or perhaps even skip definition of the emotional part of the sequel when you might go into that more deeply, thus lengthening the total sequel? In the thought portion of

the sequel, has the character sufficiently reviewed and analyzed things? Perhaps most important of all, are you sure he has considered all the next-action options he might realistically consider in his present situation? If not, then you can show his further thinking about options, again lengthening the sequel and slowing the reader down.

You might even be able to come up with so many new options—none of which looks very great to your character—that he could get frustrated, scared or angry about his plight—so that he could have moved out of his emotional stage of the sequel and then find himself *right back into it again* as a result of trying to think logically and seeing more clearly than ever what a mess he is now in.

Also, please note that there is nothing at all wrong with building in more story time between the decision on a new action and the sequel-closing new action itself. You see this sort of thing happen most often in detective or crime fiction, where the police officer hero, for example, decides that next he has to find and interview Madam X—but he's on special assignment for the next few days and won't have time to look her up, and then when he does have time, he has to go check several addresses and ask several sets of questions of other people before he can find her. (Some of these might turn into scenes unless you watch out, so be sure to *summarize* all such questionings, stressing that it's a long, wearying process, all this dull footwork poor Sam Spade is being forced to do as he struggles ever so slowly and tortuously to be able to get into that next scene with Madam X!)

7. *In extremis*, you may even wish to consider slowing the pace by changing the nature of some of your existing scenes so that they don't really function well as scenes any longer. How would you do this? By doing such ordinarily terrible things as letting the hero wander into a confrontation with no clear-cut idea of what he wants next . . . or by having the "antagonist" turn out to be friendly and mildly helpful—and therefore dull and slow to read about . . . or by making the scene-ending disaster so subtle that the viewpoint character simply walks away in a state of befuddlement.

You can get double duty out of this last-described gambit. If the fact that there has been a disaster at the end of a scene or semi-scene, but it does not dawn on the viewpoint character at the end of that scene, then he certainly is not going to be pushed into any swift action. At the same time, as he goes into a very mild sequel, you can then have him review and suddenly realize that—"Wait a minute, I just experienced a disaster and didn't know it at the time!"

Thus, in terms of the reader's perceptions, you have done all the following: (a) calmed and slowed the scene; (b) removed all need for quick response by the viewpoint character at the end of it; (c) greatly expanded the slower-moving sequel by—in effect—forcing your character (and your reader) to wade through slow-moving review and analysis before the previous disaster is even perceived.

When you pull off a trick like this, in terms of reader perception you have actually *moved the disaster into the middle of the sequel* because it's only then that anyone realizes a disaster has taken place. I guarantee you that if you use this technique, your story pace will slow dramatically: Your hero will be under less time pressure, your sequels will get longer, and the total impact of your scenes and semi-scenes will seem less forceful in terms of requiring swift further story line development.

Thus—whether your story pace is too slow or too swift—you can remedy matters once you thoroughly understand the nature and structure of scene and sequel.

At this point, however, I must admit to some personal qualms about having given nearly equal time to ways to speed up or slow down a narrative. That's because in my experience of teaching fiction technique in the university classroom for more than two decades, novice novels that fail because they move too slowly outnumber those that move too fast by a margin of about 10 to 1.

There seem to be at least five obvious reasons why this should be so:

1. As explained before, too many beginning writers unconsciously shy away from presenting conflict just as they shy away from conflict in real life. Few of us like the emotional discomfort of a nasty fight in real life, and there is a danger that we might try to dodge conflict in our fiction, too, for the sake of "comfort."

2. Too many beginners focus on the interior life of the character's thoughts or feelings, failing to understand the reader's yearning for *outside* action of some kind, played onstage in the story "now."

3. Most beginners start out with little concept of how many plot events (scenes) it takes to construct a story of 60,000 or more words. They start with half—or a fourth—of the amount of "scene stuff" they are going to need, then try to pad out to novel length by writing padded sequels.

4. Writing scene conflict is hard, both in terms of handling the terse writing style involved and in terms of the emotional fatigue such writing brings upon its creator.

5. Too many beginners want to be "poetic" or "philosophical," so they write overblown sequels to wax rhapsodic about character emotion, or bombast about their profound ideas.

It is even possible—believe it or not—to make a novel read too slowly *by making too much of your scenes.* By this I mean taking the idea of moment-by-moment narration to a painful extreme. Again, such minutely detailed overwriting may be the result of the writer's suddenly panicking when she realizes that she just doesn't have enough "stuff" (for which read: a sufficient number of dramatic confrontations) to "make length" for a novel. So what she does is expand and elaborate every scene she *does* have until the reader wants to scream.

I experienced an extreme example of this kind a few years ago when

I worked with a very talented young writer who was awfully good at writing detail, but not so hot on imagining additional plot events. Unfortunately, he was also too quick to hear any advice I might give, and then take that advice to an extreme.

He was writing a novel about a man trying to stop the inadvertent launching of an Atlas missile from a silo. By the time he reached the crucial late scene where the missile was fired anyway, he was about 30,000 words too short for a novel, didn't have enough scenes to make length, and wasn't developing very well the scenes that he did have.

In his first draft, he had the hero peer out of the bushes at the missile silo site, see the doors open, and the missile shoot out and on its way— *whoosh!*—just that fast. I lectured him about "building the scene bigger" with more moment-by-moment action.

Now, the Atlas missile in the silo had the words United States of America painted on its side, vertically, reading from top to bottom. So when my under "stuffed" and too-eager-to-please-me student came back with his rewrite of that single shot paragraph, the incident now required about ten pages.

The doors swung open. They took about two agonized pages of description of motors whirring, concrete groaning, metal screeching, etc., to get open. Then the missile was fired. It's axiomatic that "time can stand still" for the character at such a moment of crisis, but what my student did was extraordinary in its extremity. The nose of the missile appeared above the surface. (One page of description of the shape and particular color of red that the tip was painted.) The first linear foot of the missile appeared as it began to rise. We saw the letter *U*. (Two paragraphs of character internalization about how terrible this was.) Next came the letter *N*. (Another few paragraphs about how awful, and what the next letter would be, and how he had arrived too late, etc.) By the time we got to the next page, out came another foot or so of the rising missile, and we saw the letter *I*. More internalization.

It took the full ten pages to get the missile out of the silo as we counted it out, letter by letter, U-N-I-T-E-D-S-T-A-T-E-S, and so forth!

This extremity of moment by moment was as slow-moving as anything these tired eyes have ever seen. The moral: You can carry a good thing to such absurd lengths that even a supposed scene or high point of action in the story gets slow and boring.

But even if you don't go to such extremes—and even if you "have enough plot"—you need to remember something that's been previously mentioned in this book. Readers today are impatient.

Even a decade or so ago it was possible to write longer and more minutely detailed scenes than readers will accept today. Compare, for example, a classic best-seller of yesteryear such as *Hotel*, by Arthur Hailey, with any of today's novels by someone like Sidney Sheldon.

Hailey's biggest books were long, fat, multiple-viewpoint novels with fully developed scenes, some of which ran eight or ten pages of book print, or even longer. Because he wrote about several viewpoint characters, and developed his scenes to such length, the time span of most of his books was very short, sometimes only a few days, in *Airport* only hours. Because he was (and is) so good at providing harsh problems in his disasters, his novels sold very, very well.

Sheldon, on the other hand, does not write such fully developed scenes today. He condenses scenes to the minimum, skips sequels, starts scenes in the middle, and performs all sorts of other tricks to make the pace incredibly swift. He has as many or more viewpoints as Hailey ever did, but because he writes so tightly, the time span of some of his books is multigenerational.

Sheldon, incidentally, has said in interviews that his first drafts are four to eight times longer than his finished books. He starts *with plenty of plot stuff* and then writes his scenes and sequels for all they are worth. But then, in search of greater and greater narrative speed, he ruthlessly and relentlessly slashes and boils his material. Sometimes he breaks most of the rules about viewpoint and everything else to tighten something a bit further.

Sheldon's structure is more in tune with today's impatient readers. Most of us are struggling to learn ways to speed things up in our books, not slow them down.

The moral of all of this? In starting out on a novel, be sure you imagine world-aplenty of material—many, *many* scenes planned, with good, developed sequels to link them. Write all of them for all they're worth, confident in the knowledge that you not only can, but almost certainly will, go back through the manuscript, adjusting many of your structural components to achieve the pace you ultimately desire.

CHAPTER 9

VARIATIONS IN THE INTERNAL STRUCTURE OF SCENE AND SEQUEL

ONE OF THE THINGS THAT MAKES IT devilishly difficult sometimes for an inexperienced fiction writer to see structural principles in action, in published copy, is the fact that there are so many possible deviations from the structural norm.

You have seen, for example, that the classic structure of the scene is goal . . . conflict . . . disaster *in that order*, with the bulk of the structure made up of the conflict component. You have also seen that the classic structure of sequel is emotion . . . thought . . . decision . . . action, also *in that order*. And although we've looked at methods of tinkering with the length or intensity of internal components for good reason, or even leaving out a part of a sequel, for example, for reasons of narrative pacing, we have not previously considered the possibility that parts might sometimes be presented out of their normal order for some good dramatic reason, or that other variations might occur such as a flashback scene that might "play" inside the thought compartment of a sequel, or a scene which might have so little time pressure on it that a viewpoint character's momentary internalization takes on the structure of a full-fledged sequel right in the middle of things.

This is all difficult enough, but it's just the tip of the iceberg. However, for you to understand more fully all the permutations of scene and sequel structure, it's necessary to look at some of the more common deviations from the classic internal structure so that you can understand what's going on as you analyze published work, and then expand your own arsenal of structural weapons.

Before wading into this morass of variations, however, let me restate two important points:

1. A novel can be successfully written in the straight, classic scene-and-sequel structure you now know, both in terms of the *internal structure* of each scene and sequel and in terms of the *larger sequential structure into which the scenes and sequels are arranged*, Scene #1 (classic pattern) being followed immediately by its Sequel #1 (classic pattern), followed by Scene

#2 (classic pattern) followed by its Sequel #2 (classic pattern), and so on, all the way to the climax of the book.

What does this mean to you the author? Simply that you already know enough to produce a narrative structure that's entirely salable in today's markets.

2. If you have good plot reasons for doing so, you may depart from these classic structural patterns. But no matter how far you wind up straying, in the structure of your final manuscript, *you should plan your story originally in classic scenes and sequels, arranged in the classic straight sequential pattern, with nothing skipped anywhere and no part of anything out of its normal order.*

To put this another way, what I'm saying here is that you plan, basing your whole book's architecture on Scene #1 – Sequel #1 – Scene #2 – Sequel #2 – Scene #3 – Sequel #3, etc., with every part in its natural order, nothing left out, and no variations of any kind. *Then,* having laid out your entire story blueprint, maybe you will want to introduce some variations for good reasons.

Having said that, we can turn now to a more detailed look at ways you may elect to depart from the established structural norms, first in terms of scene, later in terms of sequel.

VARIATIONS IN SCENE STRUCTURE

Let's look at the five major ways you can vary your scene structure.

1. You can start your presentation somewhere other than at the classic (and logical) entering point, which is statement of goal.
2. You can end somewhere short of a fully pronounced disaster.
3. You can interrupt the scene virtually anywhere by having other action intervene.
4. You can interrupt the conflict component by having the viewpoint character's internalization in response to a stimulus develop into "a sequel in the middle of things."
5. You can present the goal-conflict-disaster segments out of their natural order.

We'll consider each in turn.

1. You can start your presentation somewhere other than at the classic (and logical) entering point, which is statement of goal.

Why might you start a scene other than with the normal statement of the viewpoint character's goal? A couple of possible reasons were suggested in chapter 8. It could be that the character's goal in this scene is so obvious that it needn't really be stated at the outset. Or it might be that the goal

was so well articulated in the preceding sequel decision that it doesn't
have to be stated again right away.

Suppose, for example, that a scene just ended in which our hero, an
Indiana Jones type, struggled with the villain and as a disaster was hurled
backward to fall through a hole in the floor into a pit of snakes. This kind
of disaster allows no time for a sequel, and Indiana's new goal is pretty
obvious: *Get outta here!* This new scene would hardly need to articulate
the goal; our hero would simply start fighting the snakes and/or looking
for a way out.

Or suppose you have just had a long sequel in which your hero has
decided that his next goal-oriented step must be to patch up the quarrel
with girlfriend Jill. This is carefully stated as his new decision-goal. We
now start the scene with him appearing at Jill's door, a beautiful bouquet
in hand. Can anyone imagine that he has to state his goal immediately
when we already read about it in the preceding sequel and have evidence
of it now in the bouquet?

There is a third obvious reason for starting a scene somewhere other
than with the goal statement, however, and here again we get into seeming
paradox. We might plunge straight into the conflict portion with the
goal—and even the stakes—unclear at the outset *with the express intention
of shocking and momentarily confusing the reader*—getting him to sit bolt up-
right in his chair, disoriented and off balance, saying, in effect, "Wait a
minute, what's going *on* here?"

This can be a useful device if not overdone. Once in a while it can
be used with devastating effect in terms of hurrying your story along and
giving the appearance of a great and unexpected twist in the action.

As an example: Midway through a suspense novel I'm currently
writing, the hero of the story must slog along through several conversa-
tions with murder suspects; he has to go through these scenes—all conflictful but none *highly* dramatic—to learn some crucial information that
next sends him to interview a doctor. Each of these brief scenes is presented in classic order. I began to worry that the story's pace was beginning to bog down, and that readers might start getting bored. Therefore,
in moving into a new chapter that was to start with the hero interviewing
the doctor, I chose to jump well into the new scene—halfway through, as
a matter of fact—with my hero already reacting in shock to what he had
already learned.

So the *first draft* of the new chapter began something like this:

> "Doctor Johnson," Bradley said, "I hope this won't take more than a
> few minutes. I know you're a busy man. But I've got to know what that
> physical exam showed."

All well and good—and rather routine in terms of pacing and structure.
So the *second draft* leaped into the middle of the scene, with a new chapter
opening with the following words:

> Bradley jerked back with shock. "Are you telling me the exam *didn't
> test* for drugs?"

Johnson's eyes looked like slate. "Was there any reason for the clinic to do so at that time?"

"What *did* you test for? Why was he here?"

Faster, I feel sure you would agree—and also momentarily upsetting to the reader, who surely will be jolted out of any somnolence by the unexpected, the disorienting. There are few things as likely to regain your attention as the realization that you suddenly aren't sure where you are, or what's happening.

One warning about this last device, however: Even used sparingly, it calls for some later explanation of what the goal was at the outset—and why—and where we are now. You can fascinate your reader with puzzlement *only so long*, and then if you don't supply the structural component he instinctively knows should be there—in this case a goal to worry about—he will give up on your story in disgust. Also, readers like to be puzzled and thrown for momentary losses, as this device will do, *only so often*. Then they'll get tired of constantly wondering what's going on, and they'll recognize what you're doing to them—creating artificial momentary suspense by withholding information they ordinarily would already have. At this point you've overdone a good thing and lost your reader. In my draft manuscript mentioned above, I use this particular speed trick twice in a 90,000-word novel.

How do you show later what the withheld goal was at the outset? Maybe you allow your viewpoint character to restate his opening goal—the one you haven't started with this time—during the course of the conflict. This is likely, actually, because strongly motivated characters tend to restate their scene goal several times, perhaps even in the same words, several times during the playing out of conflict. If, on the rare occasions when the goal does not become clear through this kind of restatement, it will become apparent only when we see what kind of disaster finally befalls our hero.

The point to remember here is that however it happens, the goal must be made clear at some point not too far down the line. The reader has to know, ultimately, what was intended and at stake, even if he's told only after the fight is over.

Here is the next way you may deviate from classic structure:

2. You can end somewhere short of a fully pronounced disaster.

How would this work? Suppose that you have set things up earlier in the story so that the reader knows something that the viewpoint character in this scene does not know. For example, the reader might earlier have been in the viewpoint of the antagonist, and heard him say that he intended to trick the hero, in their next confrontation, into coming out to the country house where hero can be ambushed and kidnapped. *Now,* with the reader knowing this, we see the heroic viewpoint character walking into the scene with the goal of getting the old family papers from his brother-in-law, the villain of the piece. They argue about this. At the end of the conflict, the brother-in-law throws up his hands and says something like, "All right! You can have the damned papers! They're out at the country house. We'll go get them right now."

This varies from normal structure in that the viewpoint character has no sense of disaster, so that the scene seems to stop short of any kind of disaster. It's seen as a *"Yes, but!"* disaster only in the eyes of the reader, who in this case has more information than the character does.

You can go even further than this, actually, with sophisticated readers. They don't know that every scene ends with a disaster. They don't know the terminology, much less the technique. But they know to expect the worst at all times. So, in the scene example given just above, most of your readers would be instantly suspicious of trickery ahead—the existence, in other words, of a hidden disaster here—even if they hadn't gotten any previous information about the villain's plans. This is a wonderful thing about fiction readers. They'll worry sometimes even when you don't add the disaster, because *they know it's there somewhere.*

3. You can interrupt the scene virtually anywhere by having other action intervene.

This third variation is a device that seems to be used a bit more frequently than either of the first two. Here are some examples of how it might work:

• Viewpoint character walks into office of antagonist and states his goal for the scene. Some other character walks in or calls on the telephone and gives one character or the other some new information, or starts her own scene with either of them; or perhaps—*rarely*—accident intervenes: The telephone call says the antagonist's wife has had an accident, and so this scene we've just started will have to be postponed.

Why would you choose to do something like this? Usually as a device to introduce additional temporary suspense. Having been told the scene goal, your reader will have already formed a scene question, which he will now worry about until the conflict plays and the question is answered.

• The scene is under way and the fight is on. But—again—another character intervenes so that her scene takes momentary precedence over our original scene. You have a scene-within-a-scene, and probably our main scene will not get to play out to its conclusion until the interrupting scene has concluded. Sometimes this device is necessary to jog the original scene's conflict pattern out of circularity, or change the motives of one of the antagonists a bit; the disaster ending the scene-within-the-scene could be such that either our viewpoint character or his antagonist would suddenly find himself standing on different ground than he occupied before new action interrupted the ongoing conflict.

You will find further discussion of this particular technique in chapter 13. You may, however, wish to turn now to Appendix 6, where an example of this strategy is given. The situation there—briefly—is that the author needed to change the motivations of the viewpoint character on a moment's notice during the unfolding of a scene; she had to accept a date with a character whom she ordinarily would not agree to see again; to motivate her to *accept* the date, the author brought in another character, initiated a fight between this interloper and the viewpoint character—and had her decide to accept the date with the other man to spite the man who had just come in and started a scene-within-her-scene.

4. You can interrupt the conflict component by having the viewpoint character's internalization in response to a stimulus develop into "a sequel in the middle of things."

This scene structure variation can be very useful, but paradoxically you may find that it tries to happen all the time during your scenes, and you have to keep fighting to *prevent* its happening too often.

Here's why. You already realize that the internalization within a stimulus-response transaction and a sequel between scenes are two demonstrations of the same underlying dynamic.

The stimulus-response pattern: External action (small); internalization (small); new external action (small).

The scene-sequel-scene pattern: External action (big); sequel (a big internalization); new external action (big).

So, because the basic dynamic is identical in the two kinds of transactions, what happens during harshly conflictful scenes is that various stimuli sent by the antagonist are so powerful and upsetting to the viewpoint character that his momentary internalizations tend to want to get out of hand and grow into virtual sequels. *Most of the time you can't let this happen;* the show (the scene) must go on. Often you will find yourself saying, in effect, "Hal Hero really wanted to have a sequel here, but he just didn't have time. Instead, he responded, 'You're wrong, J.B.! I—' " (Etc.)

To put this another way, one of the things you have to work hard on, when your scenes are really going well, with strong stimuli flying, is keeping internalizations under control so that they don't grow into sequels.

Which is why it's relatively easy to let a sequel happen in the middle of a scene if and when you believe it might be tactically desirable. All you have to do sometimes is have the antagonist hurl a particularly brutal stimulus, and your viewpoint character can plunge into an internalization so well developed that it is, for all practical purposes, a sequel inside a scene.

Why would you want to do this? Often, it's to make sure the reader is fully in tune with the thoughts and feelings of the character as the scene is playing out. Sometimes it's to have the character remember some background information that wasn't worked into the story earlier. Sometimes it's necessary to explain, ahead of time, why the viewpoint character is about to pull some unexpected gambit or seem to change his scene goal a bit, or try an unexpected scene strategy.

As mentioned earlier in a different context, your reader will sometimes accept these moments in the story when present time stops, and it's as if the characters stand frozen, in a twilight zone, while the viewpoint character's mind races through internalization. But as with all these variations, if you overdo it, the reader will get sick of it. To be used sparingly, and only with good plot reason!

5. You can present the goal-conflict-disaster segments out of their natural order.

Here the reader can be plunged into the scene very late in the conflict segment; then the disaster falls, but it's only as the viewpoint character tries to continue the scene, reiterating what he *wanted*, as opposed to what he's gotten, that we fully appreciate either the goal or the scope of the disaster. So that the pattern of the entire scene might look like this: *conflict* (already well under way)—*disaster* (not entirely clear)—*more conflict* (as the viewpoint character tries to continue fighting, during which time he finally restates the)—*goal*—followed by the antagonist repeating the *disaster*.

And in fact professional writers use most of these variations at one time or another, and ring up all kinds of changes and permutations on them. A sequel-like long internalization will stop the present scene dead in its tracks; then, during the interrupting sequel, the hero remembers some previous scene, *to which he then flashes back with the result that some of it seems to play onstage in the story "now."* At which point the viewpoint character comes back to the present and continues *this* fight, at which point another character rushes in and interrupts this scene again with her new scene, and so on and so on.

Complicated? Yes. Confusing? Not necessarily. You can always get back on track after a structural variation if you just remember where you left the classic structure, and return to the same point. The potentially chaotic mishmash of segments interrupting other segments, such as the scene-in-sequel-in-scene-interrupted-by-scene just described above, for example, would work just fine as long as the writer remembered to return to the ongoing conflict segment in the current scene after she has done all her wandering around. But confusion would come in a hurry if she forgot where she had left the track, and came back to the present in, say, some other scene a day later—or in the middle of the viewpoint character's sequel to some later scene which had also been skipped.

There is, to be sure, a danger the reader might get confused. The writer who uses all sorts of variations on the standard scene structure must often rewrite and rewrite again, focusing on the viewpoint character's *primary worry and preoccupation* at the present time in the story, so that the author can show clearly how the various deviations from normal scene structure are tied into the story through the character's interpretation of them. As just one example, a character might be thrust into the middle of a scene which might make little sense unless the author kept reminding the reader that *information about the crime is badly needed*; then the character might—in the middle of this scene seeking information—flashback to some previous episode; although the previous episode might be played as a scene-within-a-scene, the reader will not be confused if the author pauses a few times during this segment to reiterate the character's preoccupation with his need to *collect information*.

What does all of this mean to you the writer? It means that you can deviate from the norm in scene structure if you have good reason to do so. But you should always plan everything in the straightforward, normal scene-sequel pattern first. Every deviation from the norm puts extra stress on your talent and ability to maintain the reader's focus and story-orientation.

VARIATIONS IN SEQUEL STRUCTURE

Because it does not demand tight, moment-by-moment development and is loosely organized around the ever-changing feelings and thoughts of a viewpoint character, sequel may vary in structure in an almost limitless number of ways. We will consider only the most common variations, which are as follows:

1. You can skip one or more parts, or portray a segment in only a word or two.
2. You can amplify any given portion out of all proportion to the others.
3. You can mix up the normal presentation order of the component segments—i.e., emotion, thought, decision, action—if there is reason to do so.
4. You can interrupt a sequel with the unexpected onset of a new scene.
5. You can insert one or more remembered scenes within the thought component.

Let's look at each of these in turn.

1. You can skip one or more parts, or portray a segment in only a word or two.

This point was mentioned earlier in the context of how much any given scene should be developed. A sequel, too, may be lengthened or truncated, depending on the type of story you're writing, the kind of viewpoint character you're "in" at the moment, and the general level of immediate pressure on the character will help determine whether you should skip or gloss over a portion of the sequel, and, if so, how much cutting should be done.

A general rule might be stated as follows: The more painful the preceding disaster, the more fully developed the resulting sequel should be. But this is a very general rule only. It stands to reason that a character presented with a really devastating disaster will need more time to get through his reactions and on to new action than would a character presented with a disaster of lesser proportions. But sometimes the disaster is not only a grave one, but one which presents such a pressing, immediate problem that the character simply cannot afford the luxury of thinking about things in a developed manner: New action is required *now.*

How, for example, are you going to write a fully developed sequel to a disaster like the following?

> Waist-deep in the freezing water, Bill swung at Simpson and missed. Simpson stepped forward and caught Bill off balance, knocking him over backwards. Simpson instantly was on top of him, holding his head under the water.

The new goal—to get out from under the water—is obvious. There is simply no time to laboriously go through Bill's emotions, thoughts and rationale for a new decision. About the *most* you will present in a "sequel" to such a disaster will be something like this:

> Terrified, Bill clawed at Simpson's hands. There was no time to think. He simply had to get free *now* or he was a dead man.

And this is not as tightly as you could write this mini-sequel, you will notice. For, as brief as it is, it is a bit more than a simple internalization—which it very closely resembles—because it does include all the classic component parts of a developed sequel, although obviously supercondensed and out of their normal order.

2. You can amplify any given portion out of all proportion to the others.

If, for example, you suspect at some point in your manuscript that you need to work on reader sympathy for a viewpoint character, you may then elect to work extra hard and long on the emotional portion of a sequel; emotions are universal, and if you can get your reader intensely in touch with your character's emotional state, you will make your reader feel much like the character is feeling at the same time. This leads to identification with the character, and sympathy follows.

In a similar way, you may be at a point in the manuscript where you know you need to review story events for the reader. One of the best ways to do this is by having the character review them. He would do this in the thought segment of a sequel, laboriously reviewing, analyzing, and trying to plan ahead. Or the new decision that is reached might be for a complex plan that involves not only specific ideas for the next goal-motivated action, but plans for other possible scenes later down the road. In portraying all this, and showing the character's logical reasons, you might find that what is often a simple statement of goal could become a multipage statement. Would such a development of your structure worry you? It shouldn't—you still know where you are and what you are doing in terms of structure—you have simply varied from the norm for good reason.

3. You can mix up the normal presentation order of the component

segments—i.e., emotion, thought, decision, action—if there is reason to do so.

This was already illustrated in the very-brief little sequel about Bill finding himself being held underwater. The usual sequence has been changed, partly to signify swift action and some confusion in Bill's mind.

For another example, let's consider a hypothetical plot situation in which Michael has been having an argument with his friend Chuck, as a result of which Chuck (a sick man) gets angrier and angrier—and finally as a result of the stress of conflict keels over in a dead faint. (This comes perilously close to being an illogical disaster, but bear with me for the purposes of illustration.) In such a case, Michael's sequel might very well go something like this:

> (*Action*) Michael rushed to kneel beside Chuck and press his fingers against his friend's carotid artery. Chuck's pulse fluttered with crazy irregularity.
> (*Emotion*) Suddenly sick with fear,
> (*Action*) Michael ran to the telephone and dialed 911. Waiting for someone to answer,
> (*Thought*) He realized that the argument had brought on this apparent heart attack.
> (*Decision*) Now he had to keep Chuck alive until help could arrive,
> (*Thought*) But he knew he didn't have the knowledge to do so.
> (*Emotion*) His fear intensified.
> (*And so on.*)

But note, please, that in order to write such a sequel, disorganized to some degree to portray the confusion of the situation, it had to be planned first in the classic order, i.e.—

> (*Emotion*) Suddenly sick with fear,
> (*Thought*) Michael realized instantly that it must be a heart attack, brought on by the argument.
> (*Decision*) He had to keep Chuck alive.
> (*Action*) He knelt to check his friend's erratic pulse, then ran to the telephone and dialed 911.

4. You can interrupt a sequel with the unexpected onset of a new scene.

This variation does not require much elaboration this far into our discussion. Why would you rudely interrupt a sequel in this manner?

- To speed up the pace of the manuscript.
- To prevent the character from having time right now to figure something out that you want him puzzling about a while longer yet.

- To show an intensification of pressure on the character via interruption by outside influence.
- To vary from the usual structure just to keep your reader off balance.

If you employ such an interruption in your story, however, please remember what was said before about deviations of this nature. Your reader may not know a scene from a turnip, *but he has learned to have a strong sense of structure* whether he knows it or not. By interrupting a sequel, you may gain one of the advantages just listed. You may also temporarily increase the reader's "pleasant discomfort" as he fidgets, wondering (consciously or unconsciously) how this sequel is going to turn out when we can get back to it. But to keep Mr. Reader happy, and satisfy his yearning for structural completion, you must show the rest of this sequel at some point, or at the very least have your character think about how it concluded, or tell someone else in the story how it concluded.

5. You can insert one or more remembered scenes within the thought component.

Such remembered scenes can be either from background that took place before the present story began on page 1, or from events that this particular character witnessed while offstage in the present story. Appendix 5 provides a good example of this technique, along with further discussion.

Your readers sense structure, and expect their stories to adhere to structural principles. However much you choose to vary, you will be wise to see to it that the reader's vaguely realized expectations will somehow finally be met, and that strings will not be left hanging. So even if things come out of order, scene will be shown eventually to end in disaster, for example, sequel will show character emotion and thought, and so on.

As an exercise, if you want to study variations further, consider writing a few interlocking scenes and sequels in the classic order of parts, with nothing left out or misplaced in any way. (You may already have some such scenes from work suggested earlier.) Study some of these structural units and try to figure ways you might vary from the norm. Perhaps you will want to go so far as to rewrite a few as variants.

Having done this work, ask yourself which version you like best. Why? Which was easier to write? Why?

See Appendix 5.

CHAPTER 10

COMMON ERRORS IN SCENES AND HOW TO FIX THEM

IT'S POSSIBLE TO THINK YOU UNDERSTAND scene structure, yet fall prey now and again to any of a number of common errors. Here is a partial list of things that can go wrong:

1. Too many people in the scene.
2. Circularity of argument.
3. Unwanted interruptions.
4. Getting off the track.
5. Inadvertent summary.
6. Loss of viewpoint.
7. Forgotten scene goal.
8. Unmotivated opposition.
9. Illogical disagreement.
10. Unfair odds.
11. Overblown internalizations.
12. Not enough at stake.
13. Inadvertent red herrings.
14. Phony, contrived disasters.

Whew! A list of horrors if I ever saw one. But luckily you seldom make more than one of them in any given scene, and once you've been warned to watch out for them, you can avoid them all. So let's look.

LITTLE SHOP OF HORRORS

As I thought about No. 1, "Too many people in the scene," an old Henny Youngman gag ran through my mind. Man holds his arm over his head and tells his doctor, "It hurts when I do this." Doctor: "Then don't *do* that." The advice for fixing some of the scene errors listed above might be made to look almost that stupid:

You: "I've got too many characters in my scene. How do I fix it?"
Me: "Take some of them out."

Fortunately, we can make both the nature of the problem and the way to fix it a bit clearer than that.

How many characters are too many in a scene? In the usual scene of confrontation between story people, the fight is best understood if it's head to head—*meaning just two people*, the viewpoint character and his antagonist. Sometimes a story situation will demand that others be present—that your hero must confront the board of directors and fight *all* of them, for example—but the wise writer will set up her story scenes one-on-one whenever possible.

Why? Because if you put in more characters, you split the reader's focus on the two principal antagonists, thus confusing him. Also, other people standing around in the scene always seem to want to butt in, making it infinitely harder for you to continue with straightforward stimulus-response dialogue or action because your viewpoint character is being sent stimuli from more than one source. And there are all sorts of lesser nagging problems. If you have other characters in the scene, you have to keep shifting the focus a bit to describe how they're standing or how their expression may change or something equally bothersome from the creative standpoint.

If you check some of your own scenes and find mobs (any more than two people!) in a lot of them, try figuring out ways to get the extras off the set and playing the same scene *mano a mano*. If you can't figure out any credible way to cut the cast of your scene to just the two fighters, then consider other ways to render them dramatically invisible: Get all the bit players talking amongst themselves at the far end of the room during the party scene, for example, or have that irritating third person called to talk on the telephone across the hall—or even have your viewpoint character or his antagonist tell the rest of the people nearby to shut up and not interrupt again. Be ready to do almost *anything* to narrow the focus to just the two main people in the conflict.

Having done so, you'll find the scene not only easier to write, but probably a lot more intense and dramatic, too.

When you read the term "circularity of argument" in the list of common scene errors, it could have rung a bell for you. Very early in our discussion of scene conflict we noted that the participants can't be allowed to fall into one of those childish "Did not!—Did so!—Did not!" arguments that can go on endlessly and never get anywhere. But sometimes we can be aware of a principle, and still find ourselves failing to follow it.

It's hard, sometimes, to avoid circularity, two characters going around and around in conflict over a towering central issue. As a matter of fact, the bigger and more important the issue, the more strongly motivated the opposing sides will tend to be; and the more motivated, the more focused—so that sometimes it's in the biggest and most important scenes that you will most likely fall into fatal circularity.

How do you avoid this and still maintain focus on the scene goal?

1. You draw up a game plan for both opponents going into the scene—arguments they will use, tricks they may try, various responses they

will have ready if the opponent does such-and-so. You don't tip off either game plan ahead of time, but in the viewpoint character's brief internalizations, you can take note of it every time one gambit has failed or been stalled, and he moves to another tack. In like fashion, your viewpoint character can take note of it for the reader whenever he notices that the antagonist has subtly switched lines of argument.

2. You make sure that the viewpoint character keeps repeating his scene goal at regular intervals, but having once reminded the reader where the fight's central focus is, you allow the characters to move a bit off the straight line of development *and argue about other, related issues.*

For example, your hero might walk into a scene intent on selling the schoolteacher a set of encyclopedias. But by page three of the conflict, still remembering his goal, your hero might be defending door-to-door salespeople in general, or arguing that encyclopedias don't really go out of date inside a year, as the antagonist has just insisted. When things like this develop, the issue of the scene seems to broaden, and not become circular, while the reader's focus is kept strong.

The issue of *unwanted interruptions* was partly covered a moment ago in talking about having too many people onstage during the scene. Another common error made by thoughtless writers, however, is in allowing "fateful" telephone calls or sudden knocks on the closed door to interrupt everything. The intent of all such interruptions is to make the scene "more like real life," or to "confuse the situation." They make the scene more lifelike and confusing, all right—but not to the betterment of the scene. Unless such interruptions are to play some direct, dramatic role in the development of the conflict, they should not be allowed to occur. If you find some in your copy for no really good reason, you should slash them out and let the scene play uninterrupted.

Often it seems to the frustrated writer that handling one technique well only makes her aware of a related problem. That is often the case when you *get off the track* in developing the conflict portion of your scene. You concentrate so hard on avoiding circularity, introducing new angles in the argument, etc., that you find yourself four or five pages into the scene and off the course you planned for the scene at the outset.

Vigilance to the danger of getting off the track is constant for all of us. And it does sometimes seem that the better we get at introducing new angles, new maneuvers, new side issues, and new trial balloons in the course of a conflict, the more one of them tends to grab center stage and lead us too far afield from the central issue.

Staying *on* track during the conflict, however, is mandatory even at times when side issues are being argued. How do you make sure that you don't wander too far afield?

First and most important, always make sure that the scene goal has been stated clearly and succinctly. As you already know, this is vital so the reader will follow the struggle with a clear understanding of the scene question and how it relates to the story question. Additionally, however, if you the author keep it clearly in mind—and even have the protagonist restate it every once in a while during the conflict—you are less likely to allow the dialogue or fight to get too far off the subject.

How far should one go as a writer to make sure she stays close enough to the scene goal, while still allowing movement around it? Long ago, *before I had sold any novels,* I trusted myself to remember the goal clearly during every scene. Finally, after still another rejection slip for a novel in which I thought I had the scenes working just right, I adopted a desperation tactic: For every scene to be in the book, I wrote the goal in large letters on a 3×5 file card. I pasted these all over the wall in front of my old Underwood standard typewriter, in the sequence I planned to present them. Thus, every time I started a new scene or muddled my way through one, all I had to do to remember the goal was to look up at the wall in front of me.

Pretty silly, right?

The manuscript that resulted from this strategy was the first I ever sold. I continued to mess up my wall with new cards through quite a few more books before again trusting myself to remember. It's a stratagem I often suggest to writers who seem to stray from the track in their scene conflicts.

Another interior story-type device that helps you stay on the track—in addition to having the protagonist insist on repeating it often during the conflict—is to have the antagonist say, on a few occasions, something like:

> "I know what you want here, Archie. It's (scene goal). But you can't get it from me."

Still another device to help maintain strong central goal focus through all sorts of twistings and turnings in the conflict is to have the viewpoint character go into a few internalizations and, in effect, evaluate what's happening right now in terms of the scene goal. Sometimes this kind of issue-orienting internalization is *almost* as crudely stated as this example:

> We're getting pretty far from the question of my getting a loan, here. But if I can convince him I'm a good businessman with my sales charts, maybe achieving that aim will make him look more favorably on my scene goal.

And if all else seems to fail, consider simply having one of the characters complain aloud:

> "This isn't getting us anywhere! We seem to be straying from the subject. Let's get back to the basic question here."

Also, please note: We know that the viewpoint character is strongly motivated toward a specific, short-term goal essential to his long-term quest when he enters the scene. Therefore, he will tend to be preoccupied with this goal throughout the scene. In fiction, as in real life, people tend to interpret everything in the frame of reference of their preoccupation of the moment. This is why it's sometimes possible to make the wildest excursions inside the conflict appear to have relevance: The viewpoint character will inevitably interpret almost anything as relating back to the goal; you can show his line of thinking in an internalization, and so drag the seeming excursion far afield back into apparent relevance.

It may have surprised you a bit to see *inadvertent summary* listed among common scene errors. The demand that the scene be developed moment by moment, on a stimulus-response basis, is fundamental, right?

Indeed it is fundamental. Still, some writers tend to forget it, get lazy, or try to get by with shortcuts. Sometimes they skip a few minutes in a scene and protest that they had to, because the scene was running too long, or perhaps because "I wanted to get to the good part." In either case, the solution is not to revert to desperation summary; the key is to start your presentation later in the fight and write only "the good part."

Also, it should be noted that a lot of inadvertent summary slips in with certain grammatical constructions. Anytime you catch yourself writing words in a scene such as "later," "after a few minutes," "having thought it over," "when they finally got back to the subject," etc. All such constructions imply that some time has been skipped over.

This can become rather subtle, so let me offer just one example, first of the wrong way to present a bit of action inside a scene, then a correction:

> Tom stopped talking as Ralph walked to the window. A silence fell while Ralph stared out into the night. Almost a minute later, when he finally turned back to face Tom, his expression had changed entirely.

Now, you can see that there are several things wrong with this. The first sentence is written backwards in terms of stimulus and response. This often happens during inadvertent summary. Then the key word "later" shows that some time has been skipped. So let's fix it:

> Ralph walked to the window. Tom stopped talking and a silence fell. Ralph stared out into the night. *What's going on?* Tom wondered, puzzled and worried. He felt the seconds ticking off as Ralph remained motionless with his back turned to him.
> Finally Ralph turned back . . . (etc.)

What we have done here is fix the order in which the first stimulus and response are presented; used a short internalization on Tom's part not only to show his worry and puzzlement, *but to fill the seeming story time* while Ralph stands silent with his back turned, carefully noted the passing of time as Tom experiences it, second by second, and finally broken to a new paragraph with Ralph's turning back around because it's obviously the moment of a marked change in the conflict and it should be stylistically noted with the new paragraph.

Start your problem scene later to avoid the summarized part; slash the summarized time entirely; or fill it with new action or moment-by-moment thought by the viewpoint character. But be ever-vigilant for thoughtless lapses into summary. If you cleverly slip tiny bits of summary into a scene now and again for the sake of general speed in your story, do it very rarely, and remember that every such trick is exceedingly dangerous in terms of reader involvement. As discussed as far back as chapter 4, every summary threatens to jolt the reader out of his total involvement with the lifelike scene, and turn him instead into a detached observer of old history.

Loss of viewpoint happens in a scene when the writer:

1. Forgets where (in what character) the viewpoint is supposed to be;
2. Accidentally puts in a thought, feeling or sense impression belonging to someone other than the intended viewpoint character;
3. Does not provide any internalizations; *or*
4. Fails to provide occasional wording that clearly shows where the viewpoint lies.

Remember here that you should almost always restrict the viewpoint in a given scene to a single character. It is this viewpoint character's goal which provides the starting point and central focus of the scene. You simply cannot allow the viewpoint to get lost somewhere down the line.

Sometimes the problem is as simple as the writer forgetting who the viewpoint character is. In some detective and spy fiction, the viewpoint is very "cool," which means that the author intentionally does not go deeply or at length into the viewpoint character's thoughts or feelings. One of the reasons for this is tradition; another is author convenience, for it's easier to maintain a sense of mystery if the reader is seldom told everything the viewpoint character is thinking and feeling; another reason for such a cool viewpoint is that it tends to make the story more cerebral, chillier emotionally, and more tightly written—all ends to be desired in these categories.

Sometimes, however, in writing copy where the viewpoint is this cool, the style becomes almost objective—with very little indication of viewpoint at all. In such cases it's possible to forget. Remember that even in the coolest viewpoint writing, the reader needs some thought or feeling of the character every page or two to keep both him—and you—from forgetting where the focus of identification is supposed to be.

Often there is a strong temptation to tell the reader what someone other than the viewpoint character is thinking. But to put it as simply and bluntly as possible, you should seldom if ever do this. Remember the rationale for restricted viewpoint: It makes it easiest for the reader to enjoy the story and identify with the hero because the reader experiences limited viewpoint fiction exactly as he experiences real life: from only one viewpoint.

Look through your copy, seeking out possible slips in this area.

Failure to provide any internalizations can also lead to loss of viewpoint. Even the coolest stories, in terms of viewpoint handling, have strong stimuli in their scenes which demand *some* internalization. Write without any at all, and you not only lose track of where your viewpoint is supposed to be; you also find yourself writing about a thoughtless robot.

Failure to use constructions that show viewpoint is quite common, and, we can be thankful, easy to fix. To check yourself against possibly erring in this category, look through your fiction copy for places where you may have described a sight, a sound, a smell, some other sense impression, or a thought or emotion without making sure that the same sentence clearly stated that your viewpoint character experienced it.

Consider the following statements:

> The cold wind blew harder.
> A gunshot rang out.
> It was terrifying.

These are fine observations, but in none of them do we know where the viewpoint is. Ordinarily you should recast such statements to re-emphasize the viewpoint, thus:

> *She felt* the cold wind blow harder.
> *He heard* a gunshot ring out.
> It was terrifying, *she thought.* Or:
> Terror crept through her.

The simple act of learning to attach viewpoint identifiers in this way will not change the meaning at all, but will work wonders in solidifying the viewpoint.

Forgotten scene goal relates very closely to "getting off the track." But here we are talking about the kind of error in which not only does the action stray, so that the reader forgets the goal, but *the characters actually forget too.* This sounds impossible, but it's another manifestation of loss of author control. Often things will seem to go rather well even up to the disaster. But then the disaster—wonderfully horrible though it might be—simply doesn't answer the scene question, so that you have things like:

Scene goal: Joe wants to convince Sally to marry him.
Disaster: Mary gets angry because Joe mentioned Barbara.
Or:
Scene goal: Richard wants to get the promotion.
Disaster: Richard gets a bad migraine.

Such illogical, reader-frustrating disasters can only occur when somebody has forgotten the scene goal. Not only has the author forgotten, but evidently the character has, too. Otherwise, why would Joe let the scene end with anger about Barbara, when anger about Barbara is *not* the answer to his scene goal? Or why would Richard imagine that getting a migraine had any relevance to his quest for a promotion? These developments might be unforeseen difficulties, but they are not legitimate scene-ending disasters. *And a character who remembered his goal would know that.*

Error Nos. 8 and 9 relate so closely that they may be discussed together. *Unmotivated opposition* and *illogical disagreement* both show a faulty
vision by the author of why the antagonist is antagonistic. The antagonist
should not put himself between the viewpoint character and the attainment of his scene goal just to be nasty, or because you the author want
him to do so. The antagonist should have good background motivation
for his opposition if he is to be believable; and once he has this motivation,
he will have good arguments (good at least to him, anyway) that he will
make the basis of his disagreement.

Think about the nature of the opposition in your scenes, and make
sure there is motive for it. Examine the motive for the disagreement, and
then make sure that the antagonist bases his arguments and countermoves
on this background, rather than throwing out wild and illogical arguments
or claims that don't make sense to anyone.

As to *unfair odds*, consider this: We try in all our scenes to make the
conflict strong, so the opponent must therefore be formidable; but if you
make the antagonist *too* powerful and omnipotent at the outset, the reader
is never going to believe that your viewpoint character has a chance. And
the viewpoint character, who should be smart enough to see it when he
is up against *impossible* odds, will look like an idiot if he rushes into the
fray anyway. Make sure, as you write the sequel that sets up the next scene,
and portray the nature of the opposition, that he is powerful and perhaps
even scary; but don't make him such a "Terminator" that the scene will
lose all credibility because obviously the hero doesn't have a prayer of
reaching his stated goal going in.

Writing coaches tend to see *overblown internalizations* most often in
unpublished contemporary romance fiction, where the writer is straining
too hard to define *precisely* the emotional state of the viewpoint character,
even during the scenes. We have previously discussed how an internalization may become virtually a sequel-within-the-scene when strong enough
stimulus is provided. But beware those long, gray paragraphs that keep
recurring as the viewpoint character internalizes and internalizes and internalizes until the reader wants to scream. Follow the rules of stimulus
and response, and *keep the action moving along*. When an internalization is
clearly called for, or needed to help reestablish viewpoint, then fine. But
be aware that you can make too much of a good thing, and many manuscripts fail in part because their author got carried away on internalizations.

Scenes also fail, as noted, because *not enough is at stake*. The scene
goal should be important to both the viewpoint character and the opposition. Petty, insignificant goals lead to pale and puny conflicts. Always make
sure that the viewpoint character believes his scene goal is *important*, and
make sure the reader knows that it is. Pause now and then during manuscript revision, and if you find two people having a developed scene about
something like Andrew wanting to convince Priscilla to forgive him for
belching after dinner (unless you're being funny), look around for a bigger goal which can lead to a more conflictful and gripping scene because
the stakes won't be matches—they'll be fifty dollar gold pieces.

Inadvertent red herrings are not errors that will necessarily hurt the scene they're found in, but they can confuse the reader about the likely further development of the plot. I remember a student's novel once, for example, in which hero and villain were arguing about leadership of a search party into the mountains. The villain argued, among other things, that it was a trek too dangerous to undertake at once "because the threat of avalanches is so high right now." I read on as the expedition got under way, quite sure that there was going to be an avalanche at some point. There never was, and I felt cheated. Why? Because I had picked up an angle in the conflict and trusted the author to play fair: Mention the threat of avalanches and have the characters fight briefly about it, and you automatically make the reader pick up on the subject matter as a clue about future possibilities.

Fiction readers are *great* at picking up on such clues. They are magnificent at it. This is a great help to you when you really want to plant something during a conflict segment. But it's a two-edged sword. The reader is so eager to look ahead by picking up such pointers that you must be supremely cautious that you don't put in any false clues—red herrings—by thoughtless accident.

At the end of the list of common errors at the start of this chapter was *phony, contrived disasters*. If you think readers are good at picking up red herrings, you should see how fast they spot disasters that are phony—contrived events just to "make something bad happen" at the end of scenes. One of your most important jobs, during manuscript revision, should be to examine each and every scene-ending disaster to make sure that it not only grows out of the conflict, but that it isn't a one-in-a-million bit of bad luck, or something that no one in his right mind would ever believe could actually happen.

That's why, in defining the structure of scene earlier in this book, the term "logical but unanticipated" was used to describe the nature of scene disaster. The "unanticipated" is usually the easy part. The "logical" is harder. You don't want the reader to see what's coming a mile away, but you can't move mountains or send killer apes down smokestacks, either.

It's a hard job to conceive a scene goal that will lead to a tough conflict and end in a disaster that's not only unexpected but—and a moment's reflection by the reader—entirely logical. Doing it well is a fine art of creative legerdemain. The fact that it's difficult should not discourage you. The more you work at contriving good disasters, the better and more imaginative you will become at it. Finally, the day will come when you start writing disasters so unexpected, yet so logically an outgrowth of the conflict, and so really awful in the eyes of the viewpoint character, that you'll sit back in your chair and mentally chortle.

And when that day comes, you'll have left cheap tricks behind you and started to write stories that the reader can't put down.

CHAPTER 11

PLOTTING WITH SCENE AND SEQUEL

LET'S TAKE A FEW MOMENTS to review where we've been so far.

We started our analysis of fiction's structural components by looking at cause and effect as the principle underlying linear story development. Then we looked at stimulus and response transactions, and how they work. Then we moved into the larger fiction building blocks, scene and sequel, to see how stimulus and response transactions lie behind the moment-by-moment structure of scene, and how sequel connects scenes in a cause-and-effect fashion.

Having laid all this groundwork, it's now time to move on to some of the structural principles underlying the master blueprint of your long story, the planned sequence of story events we usually call "plot," and how scene and sequel fit to give structure to a lengthy narrative.

The first principle to remember in plotting with scenes and sequels is that the force underlying both stimulus-and-response transactions and scenes and sequels is the same: cause and effect. Something happens, and then—sooner or later, but in fiction usually sooner—something else happens as a result.

In the microcosmic stimulus-response world, the chain of virtually instantaneous cause and effect can go on for as long as you make sure that each response becomes in turn a new stimulus, like this:

> (*Stimulus*) "What time is it?" Rick asked.
> (*Response*) "Noon," Arnie replied. (*New stimulus as part of response package*) "Why do you ask?"
> (*Response*) "I'm nervous." (*New stimulus as part of response package*) "Wouldn't you be, if you were in my situation?"
> (*Internalization establishing viewpoint*) Puzzled and a little irritated, Arnie tried to read his friend's expression, but failed. (*Response*) "What do you mean, 'in your situation'? I don't know what you're talking about."

And so on, each structural part causing the next.

In the macrocosmic world of scene and sequel, each scene leads to the next, through the internalization-like process of sequel, in exactly the same way. Just as you build credible scenes by following the law of cause and effect in stimulus-and-response transactions, you build credible plots by linking scenes through the process of making one scene logically lead to the next via a linking sequel.

To put this another way, when we talk about "plot," what we are talking about, essentially, is a long series of scenes and sequels interlinked by the dynamic of cause and effect. Thus, if you can write effective scenes and sequels, you have the basic structural components to build a novel. All you yet need to learn is how to manipulate the parts you already understand, which involves essentially three areas:

1. Dramatic principles and devices you should remember as you plan your scenes and their linkages from the opening of the story (the crucial moment of change and formation of a viewpoint character's story goal) to the end of the story (the climax scene in which the story question is finally answered).
2. Weaving subplots into the main story line.
3. Scene and sequel content tricks to keep the reader worried.

I'll attempt to look at these areas one at a time, but because they interrelate so closely, you should be warned that sometimes it's impossible to discuss one principle without alluding to another.

DRAMATIC PRINCIPLES AND DEVICES

Every novelist should have one question in mind at every step of planning, writing and revising her novel: *How can I make sure the reader isn't getting bored?* For if you can keep the reader on tenterhooks, eagerly turning pages to see what's going to happen next to characters he really cares about, then you have succeeded as a fiction writer.

Now, there are probably some authorities around who would contend that wonderful characterization is the key to keeping the reader on the edge of his chair. Others might argue that a strong story theme is what primarily fascinates. Still others might suggest that high story stakes, or colorful locale, or richness of research background, or some other aspect keeps the reader glued to your story. These are all good ideas, but my own opinion — obviously — is that readers are initially interested, then held enthralled, and finally satisfied primarily by excellent handling of narrative structure.

Solid handling of mega-scale structure — how cleverly and well you arrange and develop your scenes and their linking sequels — gives you a framework in which story happenings can be presented in their most fascinating and suspenseful way. It also provides the framework in which you can best develop your characters, for the heart of every scene is conflict, and in fiction conflict not only reveals character, it virtually *creates* character as the story person is tested again and again in harrowing struggle — and disastrous developments which might destroy a lesser character.

Further, a well-organized story with inexorable forward movement—inevitable if the scenes are working right—will sweep the reader
along like a raftsman being carried pell-mell down a rushing river; there
will simply *be no place where the reader can relax and hop off.* Well-thought-
out sequels, arranged properly in your story, will provide not only impec-
cable story logic, but a depth of vision into every character who is given a
viewpoint.

Good structure, in other words, is in my opinion the key to getting
every other aspect of your fiction right. A few specific principles underlie
such good structure.

Probably most important in the matrix of ideas underlying sound
novel structure is the concept of what literature teachers sometimes call
rising action. By that they mean story action which seems to become more
and more intense, more and more affecting, more and more involving,
somehow, with each succeeding major development. We talked earlier
about the need to build scenes around crucial issues. But now, in addition,
if we are to be sure we have rising action, we need to make certain that
the reader's tension in scene 20, say, is higher than it was in scene 10, and
that the tension generated in the reader by scene 10 was greater than that
built in scene 5.

This is another of those "easy to say, hard to do" operations. But if
your scenes are arranged in the correct—i.e., most dramatic—order, so
that each disaster puts your major viewpoint character deeper into trouble or seemingly farther from his story goal, then that character's desperation and worry will intensify. At the same time, the reader's worry and
tension will increase proportionately, assuming you've achieved reader
identification with this viewpoint character.

And how do you achieve such identification? First, as outlined earlier
in this book, simply by establishing the viewpoint. Second, by making sure
to make clear that the viewpoint character's story goal is vitally important
to him. And third, by being careful to assure that this story goal is one
that your reader can sympathize with, and also see as important.

Thus good arrangement of your scenes to tighten the noose around
your viewpoint character's neck, combined with thoughtful handling of
viewpoint and story goal, will put you well on your way to achieving rising
action in the plot.

A plot with scenes arranged in the most dramatic order will work in
one of the following ways:

1. *The scenes will move the viewpoint character farther and farther away
from any quick shortcut to the original goal.* (Remember the old woman and
the pig?)

In such an arrangement, your character from an earlier chapter who
wanted to climb a mountain might find himself ten scenes into the book
trying to get his brother to lend him fifteen dollars *so that* he can put some
gas in his car *so that* he can drive to Dallas *so that* he can get copies of his
military records out of a bank safe-deposit box there *so that* he can hurry

back to Oklahoma City *so that* he can prove to the credit bureau that he has a valid GI insurance policy *so that* he can get a cleaned-up credit report *so that* he can make a new appointment with the banker *so that* he can go back and reapply for the loan *so that* he can start assembling climbing gear *so that*—well, you get the idea. Your hero has been working his fool head off, meeting disaster after disaster and trying again and again, and the further he goes into the story, the further he seems to be away from the attainment he really seeks. He *thinks* about this, and feels increasingly frustrated and scared with each new development moving him further away from a straight line to the mountain. The reader worries and gets tenser, too. But your character keeps going, doggedly moving backward. Your reader admires him for his tenacity—and worries all the more.

2. The scenes will develop through a series of disasters which heap new and unexpected woes on the character's head, but do not obviously relate to one another.

With this kind of development, the character is not moved so much along lines of increasing distance from, and immediate relevance to, his story goal. In this kind of story tightening, most of the disasters are not delays or new, temporary side-shoot plot vectors, as just above, but truly new and more pressing immediate trouble.

In this kind of arrangement, by scene 10 your wishful mountain-climber may find himself in a rotting jungle jailhouse in the Central American highlands *because* he was mistaken for a drug cartel kingpin *because* he flew into the local airport *because* he had to find his missing brother *because* he learned his brother was missing when he went to New Orleans to visit him *because* his brother called to say he was ill *because*—again, you see how this works.

One example of such development can be found in the John D. MacDonald novel *Cinnamon Skin*. Starting out to solve a murder, Travis McGee later finds himself in Mexico, where the disappearance of a woman suddenly forces him to abandon his original quest for a time and search for the missing person—and those involved in her disappearance. The relationship between the original story line and the Mexican adventure is tenuous, at best. It only works because Travis realizes that he has to work through the new, more pressing problem before he can get back to the old.

Now, on the surface, the two techniques we've been discussing here—backward development and the piling on of entirely new sources of trouble—seem similar. They are in the sense that both put the viewpoint character further from his ultimate goal. But in the one case, if he can ever get the first domino to fall, he may make a lot of progress very fast, just as the old woman did with her pig. But in the second case, the new disasters that have taken him further and further afield are not obviously related in a domino-falling relationship; our hero may escape the Central American jail and be no closer than that—still several disasters separated from getting back on what looks like the right track.

3. The scenes will develop in such a way that the hero must take on some entirely unrelated, shorter-term goal-quest to clear the decks for an eventual return to the original story line.

Here's an example wildly exaggerated to make the point clear: Your hero started out wanting to climb the mountain. But when he goes to see the banker, the banker tells him, "I don't have time even to discuss this right now. My daughter has been missing for three days and I'm worried sick." Our hero decides to try to help, because in this scenario his young daughter went to school with the missing child. He starts asking questions, is slugged in an alley and left for dead, gets patched up and heads for a mountain cabin that he knows the banker's family sometimes rented, and . . . It's a long time before he gets through all this subplot and back to the bank loan officer.

4. The scenes will be arranged in an interleaved pattern with scenes representing other plots — subplots — most of which will relate in some distant way to the central quest, but some which may not have anymore obvious link than the fact that they are playing out in the same setting at the same time.

In such development, the viewpoint moves around in the story, our main hero's viewpoint clearly dominating, but the spotlight swinging regularly to other viewpoint characters with strong problems of their own. Your reader will tend to get interested in all the story lines if the characters are generally sympathetic, and have their own goals. Every time the main viewpoint character strikes a particularly bad snag (disaster), making the reader most intensely interested in what is going to happen next, the viewpoint switches to one of the subplot characters until the reader gets re-interested in *that* story line, at which point this viewpoint character, too, encounters a page-turner of a disaster — at which point the viewpoint swings to someone else again, or back to the main story line.

This kind of interleafing of story lines radically slows the reader's progress through a longer story simply because there is so much more to read. This slowing-down in itself creates some additional reader tension. Furthermore, there is a cumulative effect of intensifying reader interest as more and more viewpoint characters struggle and meet with disasters, and rise to fight again. This accumulation of reader worries makes him tighten still further, turn the pages faster — and lose some sleep tonight because he "couldn't put it down."

5. Scenes can be arranged under a plot assumption that puts a clear-cut time limit on the story action — a deadline which must be met — so that a clock is always ticking.

And with every tick of the clock, the reader gets tenser — the story has better rising action — *because time is running out*.

As you recognize how well this principle leads to rising action, you may be amazed to notice how often published novelists plant some bit of business or otherwise unnecessary plot assumption to *set up a ticking clock*. Once such a clock is ticking and time is running out, the action rises intensely as both the viewpoint character *and* the reader sweat worse and worse—whether it's a time bomb hidden somewhere in the courthouse and set for 3 o'clock or the heroine's impulsive decision that "I'll force him to make his intentions clear during our date tonight—or else!"

6. The scenes will be arranged so that options dwindle.

Here, as the character tries first one thing and then another—reevaluating remaining options open to him in various sequels—the author makes it clear that first there may be ten things that might still be tried to get to the story goal . . . but later the character sees that there are only five options left, after five have already failed . . . and later, "If *this* doesn't work, there are only two things left I can see to try, and they both look miserable to me. If they both fail, what am I going to do? Will it mean I'm *finished*?"

7. Plot complications and potentially terrible developments previously hidden from the reader can be revealed.

Here, in effect, has been an author holdout. For example, *the author* might know quite well, in planning her story, that some character who seems like a minor player in the early parts of the book did some terrible deed ten years before the time of this novel, and now he is himself like a ticking time bomb, slumbering innocently—as far as the viewpoint character and reader can know—until, at the end of some scene, this hidden ogre's longtime vendetta crashes into the present story to make things infinitely more complicated for the hero than he had previously guessed.

This brings us to another general point about dramatic plotting which the beginner often overlooks in focusing so hard on the plot developments she intends to show onstage, in the story "now": every narrative is really composed of three parts: the backstory, the present story and the hidden story.

The *backstory* is everything that took place before you started page 1. Sometimes you must imagine many years of development before you have set up all the factors that will make the present range war or star-crossed romance "work right." In planning one of the early novels in my Brad Smith suspense series for Tor Books, for example, I had to go back two generations in a family and plot out crucial things that happened to the parents of my heroine as well as her grandparents before I could start chapter 1 knowing that she had a lost brother she did not know of. In Appendix 5, already looked at from another standpoint, one of the functions of the sequel is to introduce a considerable amount of that backstory.

The novels of the late Ross MacDonald, especially those featuring detective Lew Archer, were rich in backstory. Their usual plot showed something happening in the story "now" that seemed insignificant; yet terrible things then began happening, only slowly was Archer able to dig back . . . back into the ghastly secret hidden so long, yet motive for all the tragedies he was currently investigating.

The *present story* is the one you write in the story "now," of course. It's the present time shown between the covers of your book.

The *hidden story* also takes place during the present time of the story action. But it is composed of things that happen to, or are done by, characters *outside of the viewpoint character's knowledge*. These are a bit like events taking place backstage while the play is going on out front for the audience. But in fiction, the hidden story must be as carefully planned, in sync with the present story events, as if you did plan to present the hidden actions.

As an obvious example, suppose you plan for your hero to walk out of a hotel building and narrowly escape death when a heavy flowerpot falls from above and smashes to the pavement beside him. In terms of what you tell the reader, or let the viewpoint character know, this is something that simply happened. But you the author must have plotted out any number of possible actions, decisions and movements in the hidden story that *you* will know who dropped the pot, how he decided to do it and why, how he got to a good vantage point for the dropping at the precise right moment, etc.

Careful planning of the hidden story must involve imagining scenes and sequels involving characters "offstage" at the moment the present story is being played on the stage. Often you must work just as hard planning and imagining these unseen story events as you do on the material that the reader will witness. You must also work hard on the timing of events in the hidden story.

As an example of why you need both kinds of planning, consider the example of the flowerpot just above. If you are to put antagonist Jason in the building and planning to drop the pot, you have to imagine where Jason was earlier in the story, how he reacted to story events in which he was seen in the present story, and what plans he made, as well as why he made them. You can't just leap in at the last instant and drop a flowerpot out of heaven. In an identical way, you must plan the timing of Jason's movements. I have seen manuscripts in which the author did not carefully time the events imagined for the hidden story, so that a character operating momentarily in the hidden story would have to get from New York City, say, to Baltimore in sixty seconds.

As a practical device to keep track of hidden story events and their timing, let me suggest that you find a large calendar of the type which shows a month at a glance, a rather large empty block being allowed for each date. Jot in notes for your present story scenes in *black* or *blue*, putting the events in the proper calendar date and, if necessary, listing various events on the same date by time of occurrence. Now plot out your events in the hidden story by using a *red* pencil or ballpoint to write them into the same calendar blocks.

If your plot is very "dense"—which is to say, if you have many events taking place on the same days—you may need to abandon the calendar at some point and fill out a sheet of paper for each day of the story. If you do this, I suggest drawing a vertical line down the center of the sheet, top to bottom, and labeling the left-hand column "Present" and the right-hand column "Hidden." I myself have gone so far as to show every hour of a really busy plot day, putting events in on both sides at the time I envision them happening.

This may seem like a great deal of work, but it will assure that you allow time for people in the hidden story to have offstage scenes if needed to motivate them, work through sequels to draw up new plans, and have time to move through space from their last present-story location to the spot where they'll pop into present-story view, dropping a flowerpot or starting an argument or doing whatever you planned for them to do.

Clearly, plotting the hidden story is vital, even if you never actually hand the viewpoint momentarily to some of the characters for whom you must plot out backstage thoughts and actions. But whether you are writing single or multiple viewpoint fiction, you can never afford to forget your important characters and what they might—or must, for the sake of your story—be doing when off the present stage.

WEAVING SUBPLOTS INTO THE MAIN STORY LINE

But let's suppose now that you will not limit your viewpoint to a single character throughout the novel. This will involve creation of subplots, because you should always remember that *every viewpoint character should have a plot or subplot*. In some cases, the subplot for "Character C" will be little more than following the main plot line and trying to help when he can. More often, however, secondary viewpoint characters should have more reason for being in the story than forming a cheering section.

This, of course, makes it all more complex. *Now* you only have to juggle the timing and motives of everyone in the present and hidden story; you must also create subplots and figure out the most dramatic ways to weave them into the story that's told onstage.

On this point here are a few observations to bear in mind:

1. In any given segment (scene or sequel) restrict your viewpoint to a single character. (This was said before, but bears repeating because of its importance.)

2. One viewpoint must clearly dominate in your manuscript. If, for example, you have 100 scenes, then major characters Bill and Dan must *not* each have the viewpoint in fifty scenes. If there were just two viewpoints, Bill and Dan, and, if Bill is your main character, seventy (or more) of the scenes should be told from his viewpoint. If you add a third viewpoint—Janis—then you will need to establish a "viewpoint hierarchy" which shows the relative importance of each character by the number of story segments given to each viewpoint. Working with our same example, Bill should still probably have the viewpoint 70 percent of the time, giving

the #2-ranked character, Dan, 20 percent and Janis, who is #3, only 10 percent.

Earlier discussion of reader identification with the viewpoint character, as well as our study of reader desire to worry about a central story question, have already shown why such a dominant viewpoint allocation is mandatory. If you start spreading the viewpoint too evenly around in the story, the reader will not only fail to identify as strongly as we wish, he will also tend to get mixed up about which of the viewpoint characters' goals is the one he is supposed to worry about most.

3. Different viewpoints should be different. They should not all hold identical opinions about everything, react to disasters in exactly the same proportion of emotion and thought, etc. For example, if one major character feels very strongly about working to improve women's rights, fine. If *several* characters tend to talk incessantly about the same issue—and with the same set of beliefs—the characters will blur together, and none of them will be believable. If one character tends to react to every setback with major emotional outbursts—tears, gestures, and long-developed internalizations and sequels—then not every other character should show the same emotional pattern; perhaps another should be very cool, and experience little strong emotion, while a third might react strongly, but control his reactions sternly so that he shows little, and forces himself not to brood during his sequels.

4. Viewpoint ordinarily should be changed only when necessary to enhance reader curiosity and suspense.

Authors sometimes switch to a different viewpoint merely to show what the other character is thinking at the moment *when revelation of that thought really doesn't give the reader anything more to worry about*. Such changes should be avoided. On *rare* occasion you may find it desirable to change viewpoint to characterize the person taking the viewpoint, or perhaps to show that secondary character's opinion of the major viewpoint character and his plight. But fully 90 percent of your viewpoint changes should be done to heighten reader tension.

5. If and when you change viewpoint, the best place to change is immediately after a disaster has ended a scene. The next-best place is in the thought portion of the sequel. Third-best is at the moment of new decision in the sequel.

If you pause a moment to remember that we are working to keep the reader on tenterhooks, you will see why changing viewpoint in the places listed above is best. Any time a disaster falls at the end of the scene, the reader turns the page eagerly, wanting to see how the viewpoint character is going to react, and what he is going to do next. If your reader turns the page and finds himself plunged into some other viewpoint, he is going to be thrown momentarily off stride, and *will read eagerly to get back to the viewpoint plight he just read about*.

If you choose to carry the same viewpoint character into his sequel before changing to another viewpoint, the best places to change them are in the thought segment or at the moment of decision. The rationale for this is not as obvious until you think about it. If you can drop out of a viewpoint at the time that character is trying desperately to sort things out, you are still in effect leaving his viewpoint in crisis. This is suspenseful for the reader. If, on the other hand, you carry on to the moment of new decision, you will then be switching to another viewpoint just as the new decision has been reached, *which gives the story a forward thrust, and the reader a potential new scene question to worry about.*

In regard to leaving the viewpoint at the moment of decision, there is also another way to worry the reader by leaving at this point. And that is by writing something like, "Then he knew what he had to do." And change point of view without telling the reader what it is that the character just decided. This kind of a holdout drives readers nuts; use it sparingly, or they'll start writing you nasty letters.

You can see, I am sure, how this device of changing viewpoint at a moment of high reader tension and curiosity creates the kind of story that's hard to put down. As you plot with multiple viewpoint, you play a suspense-game of hopscotch with your reader. You take Character A to a disaster, let us say — and immediately switch to Character B. And where do you later leave the viewpoint of Character B? Again, at a disaster, or in his thought process as he evaluates and worries, or just as he makes a new goal-oriented decision. So *now* the reader is hooked again — and again reads eagerly.

But what about returning to the viewpoint of Character A? How do you again reorient the reader's focus to him? The answer: You pick Character A up *exactly where you left him in terms of the structure.*

By that I mean simply this: If you left him at the moment of disaster, then structurally the next thing that should happen is the emotional part of his sequel, and that is precisely where you return to him. Similarly, if you left him in the middle of thought, you pick him back up again still thinking about it. If you left him at the moment of decision, you repeat that decision as the opening lines of the section where you return to him — and then immediately show him moving into new action.

By maintaining such structural integrity, you will seldom if ever confuse the reader, or give him much trouble reorienting to a viewpoint. The reader will probably have no idea that you left a viewpoint at the disaster and picked him up later at the precise moment he started his sequel, for example — the reader doesn't know structure and he doesn't know the terminology. But since the progression of parts of scene and sequel are so true to human behavior, the reader will reorient instantly, and without much trouble.

Does this mean that you always have to go back *in time* to where you left a viewpoint when you return to it? By no means, and this is another beauty of the way the structure works. You can leave a viewpoint character for quite a bit of story time — you can even move him around offstage while you're in other viewpoints — and then you can pick him up later, and even in some other place, and simply *continue his structural pattern as if there had never been a break in his viewpoint.* You can leave a viewpoint character at the moment of a disaster befalling him in San Francisco on a

Thursday, for example, and then follow one or more other viewpoints for several hours or even days. When you're ready to go back to the original viewpoint character, you don't have to "flashback" to Thursday in San Francisco. You could, if you wished, plot it so that in the hidden story he flew to Jakarta. You can then rejoin his viewpoint in Jakarta the following Monday, and the reader will have no trouble at all with the space-time transition *if you observe structural integrity*—if you open his new segment showing him still stuck in the next structural compartment he should be in, the emotional part of the sequel following the San Francisco disaster.

For the reader, it will be as if no time had passed, and the transition simply doesn't matter to him because *structurally* nothing has happened. All you would have to do is write something like this:

> Tim was still reeling with shock from the outcome of Thursday's board meeting when he walked into the Jakarta hotel the next Monday morning.

Thus the author has brought the reader back to Tim's viewpoint precisely where his viewpoint was last seen, structurally speaking. The author left Tim at the moment of disaster, and now picks him up again in the throes of his emotional reaction to the disaster (the first part of his sequel to that disaster). The transition in space and time is irrelevant; nothing has been left out in terms of logical, classic structure.

Such devices allow for a swift-moving story and heightened reader suspense while keeping complex developments clear.

SCENE AND SEQUEL CONTENT TRICKS TO KEEP THE READER WORRIED

Of course most of what has gone before centered on keeping your reader worried—glued to his chair. There are many other tricks you can play with the content of scenes and sequels which will also add to the reader's pleasant discomfort.

In a Scene

1. Drop hints about things the antagonist seems to know which the viewpoint character doesn't. This can be as simple as having the antagonist say, "I am quite aware of the rival company's plans for its new product," when the hero doesn't know diddly. This raises an ancillary question or worry in the reader's mind, and he'll mentally fuss over it for quite some time. Just remember that you have to satisfy his curiosity sometime!

2. Have the antagonist reveal something that the hero didn't know when he started the scene. This bit of bad news can alter all your viewpoint character's assumptions about how the scene might unfold—even force him to deviate slightly from his stated scene goal. This puts the hero at a decided disadvantage—which worries the reader more. For example:

"I know you came in to ask for a raise, John," the personnel manager said. "But perhaps you didn't know that we're considering downgrading your position from Level Five to Level Three."

3. Conversely, show new information in the scene which makes it clear that your viewpoint character had faulty intelligence coming in, and assumed something that is not so. Perhaps he comes in to argue for a promotion to a new job that's opening up—but learns that job is *not* opening up. Now he has to scramble around to try to salvage something in the interview, perhaps information on other jobs that may be opening.

4. Have your antagonist set a ticking clock on the duration of the scene, perhaps by saying something like, "I've got exactly five minutes to give you. You'd better make it good and you'd better make it fast."

5. Show that the stakes are higher than the viewpoint character had realized. The antagonist might reveal that a sought-after promotion involves not only a pay raise, as our hero had thought, but also a profit-sharing program and use of a company car.

6. Have your viewpoint character think about (in internalization) or even orally hint at the fact that he has more of an agenda here than the reader can be fully aware of. (This is only possible when you are writing from a very cool viewpoint, and in the preceding sequel held back some or most of the details of his plans for this scene.)

In Sequel

1. Set a clock ticking so that the character has only so many minutes to reach a decision. Some other character may set this time limit, or the viewpoint character may set it on himself.

2. In the thought segment, have the character realize whole new dimensions of the previous disaster and his present plight that he hadn't thought of before.

3. Consider having the character's emotional reaction overwhelm him, so that he plunges back into the story battle with *insufficient* thought.

4. Devise a way to insert a "roadblock" scene in the early stages of the action segment so that the viewpoint character must, in effect, have a sidebar fight of some kind to find his way back to the next scene which he sees as relating directly to his long-term story goal.

5. Hold out on the new decision, as mentioned under No. 6 in the list of scene devices just above. You write something like, "Then he knew what he had to do." But don't tell the reader.

6. Stage an interruption—an outside stimulus—which forces the character to "stop sequelizing" and meet the new threat.

You will find as you work more with dramatic narrative structure that some of the devices mentioned herein can often be spotted in published stories. You will also notice how some authors "mix and match" their techniques, using a hint of one trick and parts of one or more others. This should not discourage you. You now understand the basics and can work the same magic yourself.

CHAPTER 12

SPECIALIZED SCENE TECHNIQUES

IN THE WRITING OF A VERY LONG story such as a novel, many troublesome, hard-to-handle plot situations can arise. As we have seen, you can work through many of these by reassessing some of your plot assumptions or rearranging some of your classically structured scenes and sequels. There are other problems and story needs, however, that require a bit more invention on your part. Nearly always, the answer is not to jettison classic structure, but to know how to bend it.

We have already looked briefly at some of the ways you can alter or rearrange structural components to solve a particular problem or achieve a certain desired effect. What follows is a deeper discussion of some of those specialized techniques, and why you sometimes need to use them. Topics:

1. Scene interruption
2. Scene-in-scene
3. Scene-in-sequel
4. Scene to delay a sequel
5. Scenes started by a nonviewpoint character
6. Flashback scenes
7. Scene fragmentation
8. All-dialogue scenes
9. All-action scenes
10. Maneuver scenes against an unseen opponent
11. Multiple-agenda scenes

SCENE/SEQUEL TECHNIQUES

It might strike you as particularly ironic that the first topic on the list is *scene interruption*, when only a few pages ago I was warning you against allowing scenes to be interrupted except under very special circumstances. The warning was against *inadvertently* setting up your story situation so that an unwanted interruption seemed to just happen. Here we're dealing with a special story situation in which you *need* to interrupt a scene for thought-out dramatic reasons.

Why might you want to interrupt a scene? Perhaps to further tease and tantalize your reader. Suppose that the scene is the most crucial yet in the novel, and you feel supremely confident that the reader is hanging on every word and action taking place. Every so often it's a neat suspense trick to create some diversion which forces a temporary postponement of completion of the conflict. When this happens, your viewpoint character wants to get on with things, but is thwarted, his scene quest postponed. In a small way, he will usually experience this delay as a setback—a mini-disaster if you will—and may even have a lengthy internalization which almost becomes a sequel as he reacts. The reader, too, is disappointed when the scene is interrupted, because he has been thwarted in his desire to learn the answer to the scene question. Therefore, the effect of carefully planned scene interruption can be an intensification of suspense.

On most occasions, when you interrupt a scene, you can set up a small ticking-clock situation by having either your viewpoint character or his antagonist set a timetable for resumption of the conflict. "I'll be back in two hours!" the antagonist says, hurrying out of the office in response to the telephone call. Or, "We can't wait past midnight!" your viewpoint character reminds the antagonist. The setting of this little clock also heightens reader worry and anticipation.

Scene interruptions are most commonly caused by the intervention of some other character who emerges from the hidden story. This character brings in news or a demand for immediate action on some other, possibly related problem. On occasion, the new character who enters the scene can demand a scene of his own, right then and there, so that we have the second technique mentioned in the list above, *a scene interrupting a scene already in progress and taking precedence over it.*

The scene that plays within an interrupted scene ordinarily is not very long. That's because such an interrupting scene is seldom put there for its own sake, but for what it can accomplish. It is not often important in itself so much as it functions as a stimulus which will change the motives of a character in the main scene already under way. You have already seen how this works in an example given in chapter 9.

Given the fact that such an interrupting scene is primarily a tool or motivating gimmick, and the scene it interrupts is still the main line of the plot action, it could be deadly if the writer allowed the interrupting scene to run on so long that the reader might forget what is really at issue in the main scene. The reader's attention must not be diverted very long; his attention should be taken back into the original scene quickly, so that the cause-and-effect relationship of the new information and change of motive-behavior in the original scene is as clear as possible.

Appendix 6, just mentioned, contains a good example of a scene being interrupted by the arrival of a third party, and then a brief scene playing inside the original one with the result that a character's actions are radically changed. You may have studied this appendix earlier, but this might be a good time to review it.

The employment of a *scene within a sequel* is also usually an attempt to introduce new information. You may wish, for example, to bring in some previously unknown part of the backstory to help explain the present feeling-thinking state of your viewpoint character. You saw an excellent example of this in Appendix 5. There, you will remember, the fugitive KGB agent in Canada recalled parts of several scenes as he reviewed the backstory.

Or you may have a character alone, taking a walk late at night in sequel, let us say. His problem is so difficult, and he is so devastated by the recent disaster, that it does not seem credible that he would work through a sequel to new action anytime soon.

Often you the author must intervene in such cases, most often to give the viewpoint character a demonstration of support—or possibly poorly advised criticism—that will jar him out of the emotional segment of his sequel. In such cases, a sympathetic character walks onto the scene and gives the hero encouragement or love, and this cheers him enough to go on to trying to *think* further into the sequel (rather than continue circular feelings of woe). On other occasions when it doesn't seem that encouragement would get the job done, or your plot is such that you don't have a friendly character handy to bring onstage, you might intervene with a hostile or neutral character whose unfounded criticism jars the viewpoint character into anger that will quickly translate into wanting to get on with things.

Sometimes it's the thought portion of the sequel you need to interrupt with a scene. In such cases, the intervention of another person clarifies the hero's thinking and he sees, through the insight of the interrupting person, a new line of thinking that leads quickly to a new goal—and forward movement.

Use of a *scene to delay a sequel* usually appears on the surface like nothing more than one scene bumping front-to-back with the one that preceded it, no time being allowed for a sequel. But sometimes you the author need to delay the occurrence of a sequel to place it later in a chapter, say, perhaps at the chapter ending, where it will have more impact. In such a case, you intervene dramatically so that something *new* happens immediately after a scene-ending disaster, and tailor things so that the viewpoint character must deal with the new problem in a new scene—or even several of them—before he literally has time to experience his sequel to the initial scene.

Suppose, for example, you have a disaster at the end of a scene which calls for a sequel in which your viewpoint character very obviously is going to have to make some decision which will profoundly influence the remainder of the story. But at the same time your plot is so pressurized at this point that new events are going to transpire almost at once. If you were to present your sequel at once, it would necessarily be short, and might even have to be interrupted for credibility's sake by the onrush of additional events. And so the impact of the sequel, important as it is, might be lost in the flood of additional scenes.

It is in such a situation that the best thing to do is not to try to play the sequel in its proper order at all, but simply to allow the new scene or scenes to interrupt—saving the skipped important sequel until some time later—preferably the end of the chapter—when there is finally time for the character to go through it, and where it will attain greater significance in the reader's eyes because it will stand at the end of the chapter as a hook to future developments.

My favorite example of this technique in action is one I tend to repeat often in lecture situations. In chapter 4 of John D. MacDonald's *A Deadly Shade of Gold*, Travis McGee takes a woman to seek out a friend, Sam Taggart. Travis finds Sam, all right—dead in his motel room, his throat slashed from ear to ear.

Realistically, as the story is set up, Travis can hardly have the luxury of an immediate, developed sequel to this terrible disaster. The woman with him instantly becomes hysterical, and he has to get her somewhere for care; the police must be notified—also at once—and when they arrive, Travis must answer all their questions. All that done, he must return to the place where he left his female companion to make sure she is all right.

Only after all this has taken place in rapid-fire order does Travis *have time* to experience his sequel to the death. Heading home in the dead of night, Travis finally experiences the shock and sadness of Sam's murder in a moving passage which begins as follows:

> I walked across to the public beach. . . . The sea and the night sky can make death a small thing. Waves can wash away the most stubborn stains, and the stars do not care one way or the other.

At the end of the sequel, Travis has decided that this time the unknown killers had taken one of his own—a best friend—and he intends to find them and make them pay. This conclusion to the sequel—having been delayed for quite realistic reasons of time pressure—*now falls at the end of a chapter, where it has maximum impact on the reader*. Thus an accomplished novelist like MacDonald plays with structure to put the most important single motivating idea of the chapter—the vow for revenge—at the place where it will hit the reader hardest.

NONVIEWPOINT CHARACTER SCENES

Scenes started by a nonviewpoint character must occur sometimes in fiction, despite everything that has been said about classic structure. It would seem to be virtually impossible for a scene to start in this way, as we have consistently (up until now) looked only at scenes in which the goal is conceived by a viewpoint character and clearly stated by him upon entering the scene. Thus the implication of everything that has preceded this section of this book has been that the viewpoint character must initiate the scene with *his* goal. But while ordinarily this is true—and you want to try to a great preponderance of your scenes from the stated goal of the viewpoint character, clearly it cannot always be so: In fiction, as in real life, sometimes someone else walks in with a stated goal, thus initiating the scene.

Such situations tend to occur more often in the early parts of novels, or at times of a major transition in space. As the story is just getting under way, the central viewpoint character often is *acted upon* to get him into motion. In such cases, a scene might easily start by someone else walking in, stating a goal, and starting a scene, or by shooting at the hero, for another example, and starting a chase scene. The same tends to be true after the viewpoint character has just made a big space transition, to a new neighborhood, a new town or even a new country; he may still be getting his feet on the ground, but if you are concerned with keeping the story on the boil (as you should be!), you cannot afford to waste pages showing him walking around trying to find a hotel room. Such transitional reorientations often require someone from the hidden story to appear and start the scene sooner than the hero would logically get around to it.

Here is one example from a manuscript I happen to be working on at the moment. My character, Barton, has concluded a scene in which he received some very bad news about the business failure of a friend. Barton has already decided to call on his friend in the morning, when the friend returns from a trip to Chicago. But at this point my *author intention* is to introduce another character—and a major subplot.

Barton can't do it for me by entering into a scene with a goal, because he isn't even aware yet that the other character exists. So, back in his hotel room, after showering, he hears a knock on his door and the following scene begins from the goal-motivation of a character other than the viewpoint character:

> Barton opened the door and looked out at the slender, middle-aged man in the hallway. "Yes?"
> "Jim Barton?"
> "Do we know each other?"
> "No." A tic leaped near the man's right eye. "I'm Krohner—Frank Krohner. I have to talk to you. Can I come in?"
> Barton hesitated. He was tired and frustrated, and the last thing he needed was a stranger barging in. But Frank Krohner did not look like a kook. His suit was expensive, and so was the diamond ring on his finger. He had a straightforward way about him that Barton instinctively liked; he did not seem like the kind of man who hammered on hotel room doors in the middle of the night without good reason.
> Barton swung the door wider. "Come in. What is it you want?"
> "I want to show you some pictures."

At which point Barton lets Krohner in, and a scene develops in Barton's viewpoint, but from Krohner's goal motivation.

In all such situations, the viewpoint character immediately responds to the appearance of another character with some goal by asking or doing something in an attempt to figure out as precisely as possible just what the intruder's scene goal may be. This makes it easy for you to get the other person's goal stated. Now, having gotten the goal stated by the nonviewpoint character, you must make it clear quickly that the viewpoint character does not agree with this goal — thus setting up conflict and getting the major portion of the scene rolling.

The important difference between this kind of scene and the more normal one is that generally *you still want the disaster to befall the viewpoint character*. You can see why this should be so in terms of keeping your reader worried; if a disaster befalls a character in opposition to the viewpoint character — even when that other character started the scene with his goal — what would the effect be for the hero? If the disaster were to befall the villain of the story just because he happened to start the scene with his goal, then such a disaster would be a good thing for the hero; and we can't let good things happen for the hero for all the reasons stated as far back as chapter 4.

So the fundamental difference in the scene started by a nonviewpoint character is that the disaster must not befall him — he must to some degree *attain his scene goal* so that the tactical effect will be disastrous for the viewpoint character.

To put this another way, from the standpoint of the nonviewpoint character, the pattern of the scene is *Goal — Conflict — Success*. This in turn makes the effect of the structure on the viewpoint character look something like this: *Curiosity* (as to what the goal is) — *Conflict — Disaster*.

Of course there can be a variation even on this internal structure, when you are in multiple viewpoint. The viewpoint in a given segment of the story may be in the story villain, who is having a scene with some minor minion while the story's hero is offstage somewhere. In such a case, the villain as goal-stater in the scene should encounter disaster at the end of the scene *only if the disaster will motivate the villain to escalate his war on our hero, the usual viewpoint character*. In most such scenes, the villain should experience success at the end of the scene because that's what's bad for the hero whether he knows it or not; the *reader* will know it, and that's what counts.

If you think about this, you will realize that most scenes will still have the classic pattern because most scenes will be in the viewpoint of the story hero. Variations from the norm occur when your story tactics require the bad news for the hero to come in the form of good scene news for the antagonist.

Or to make it as simple as possible: Always end your scenes to make things worse on the hero — even if it means sometimes altering the usual pattern of scene structure.

FLASHBACK SCENES

Flashback scenes are a constant concern of many new writers, if one can judge by the number of questions asked at writers' workshops. A full-fledged flashback scene will occur in the thought portion of the sequel 99 times out of every 100 times one occurs. What happens is that the character, trying to review story events and possible new courses of action, may quite credibly remember some earlier life event which seems to have relevance.

Again, Appendix 5 takes on added relevance here. It would have been possible for me to work in the character Partek's background in other ways, the introduction of secret documents, for example. But by showing Partek in such emotional straits, I was able to have him remember earlier crucial events in some detail, making them more dramatic for the reader.

I did not present fully developed scenes, beginning to end, as part of the Partek sequel because sufficient information could be gotten across without going to such lengths in a novel that I knew was already running dangerously long—close to the 90,000-word maximum set for me by the publisher. However, if you have the manuscript space, and the past events have enormous dramatic potential, you may elect to have time flashback more fully in a sequel, and play one or more scenes moment by moment, in the classic form, while time stands still in the present sequel.

Note, however, that this can be dangerous because the reader will—you hope—get totally wrapped up in the old scene or scenes. When you bring him back to the present time in the sequel, he may be badly jarred by the transition. Also, if you get into the habit of doing this too often, your story is going to bog down in a review of old events, rather than moving forward to new ones.

Often it is more economical in terms of space, and more effective for the reader, if you can avoid the all-out flashback *scene* and instead summarize it in the sequel form. This in effect can become a sequel-in-a-sequel, or merely a lengthy internalization during the thought segment. In either case, holding to sequel structure allows summary as well as interpretation by the viewpoint character, and might be the better way to go.

It's conceivable that a flashback scene—a short one—could play during a profound internalization during a present-action scene. But this trick probably should be avoided. Your reader may have a hard time believing that "time stood still" long enough in the present scene to allow a flashback scene—with its own moment-by-moment development. And if you do this anyway, what do you do with the sequel that should logically follow the scene you just presented in flashback? *Where does it end?* Again, summary of the character's thoughts and feelings about the old scene, with the briefest description of its course, is an infinitely safer way to go.

This brings us logically to *scene fragmentation*. For often you see only a fragment of a scene—sometimes as little as a single, vital dialogue exchange—inside a present scene internalization or in the thought portion of a sequel.

Suppose, for example, you are in the middle of a scene in which your hero is trying to dissuade a friend from bungee-jumping from a bridge. A portion of the present scene might benefit from a scene fragment out of the past like the following. We're in the middle of an ongoing scene.

"Don't do it, Bill!" Richard pleaded.
Bill grinned and continued to strap himself into the bungee harness.

"Don't be ridiculous. People do this every day. What can go wrong?"

Richard froze. The words ripped him out of the present time and back to that high, windy mountainside five years earlier. Then it had been Gina on the ramp, tying herself into the hang glider.

"Gina, please don't do this."

Gina laughed at him. The strong, gusty wind tossed her dark hair. She had never looked more beautiful. "Just because you're a big scaredy-cat, darling, don't expect me to be one."

"It's too gusty today!"

She pointed out over the abyss to the soaring hang glider that had just launched. "Does it look like she's having any trouble? You're just being silly. What can go wrong?"

Then she had launched, and the wind had tipped her wings almost instantly, and she had fallen like a bird shot out of the sky.

Now here was Bill, taking a similar risk, using the identical words: *"What can go wrong?"*

The hope in all such cases where you use a scene fragment is that thrusting the reader directly back to the pivotal moment in earlier time will intensify his understanding of the character's present strong emotion or motivation, or both. It's a good device if not overdone because it does so show exactly why the character is presently so deeply involved.

ALL-DIALOGUE SCENES

So-called *all-dialogue scenes* are very common in today's fiction, and as a matter of fact nearly all the scene examples used in this book have imagined scenes in which the conflict was played out primarily in dialogue. The point to be made, however, is that so-called all-dialogue scenes must have elements other than dialogue in them to make them credible to the reader.

Obviously they must have attributions — she said's and he said's liberally sprinkled through the copy to help the reader keep straight on who is saying what. But in addition, the all-dialogue scene will probably have some internalization in it, and it will also have a certain amount of description as well as some character movement or stage action.

In keeping the reader reminded where the viewpoint is, you will use constructions such as "he saw" and "she heard," as discussed earlier in the book. Such statements throughout an all-dialogue scene will also necessarily inject some description of the scene setting, but most importantly the changes that take place in the opposing character's face. Some such descriptions can also show observation of the stage actions going on, like this:

Joe saw Adam's jaw tighten with anger, and then watched as the big man got up from his desk, started to speak, clenched his jaw as he apparently thought better of it, and then walked to the far side of the office. . . .

Such observations are vital to what is often called the all-dialogue scene. Without them, the dialogue itself can quickly become abstract: The reader not only forgets who is saying what to whom, but he also loses his ability to visualize what's going on. It's a paradox, but the all-dialogue scene sometimes takes greater care in description and viewpoint reinforcement than does a more action-oriented one. That's because it's absolutely necessary, but the fast flow of stimulus-and-response dialogue leaves you the author little space or time to work in just the right small amount.

In similar fashion, there are scenes which are *all action* in terms of the playing out of the conflict. The classic car chase is a good example wherein the viewpoint character is either chasing or being chased by another car, and he's quite alone, and dialogue is impossible. A high percentage of such an action scene is pure stimulus and response. But, as in the all-dialogue scene, continued dependence on nothing but one method of getting the point across can lose the reader; he needs something to tell him for sure what's at stake and how things are going.

How can this be accomplished? I'm sure you've already thought of the mechanism which provides the solution. A chase, say, or physical fight of some kind will be replete with give-and-take, many strong stimuli as the opponents battle. Thus it's a natural situation for internalizations to take place in response to some of the bad stimuli. It is in these brief internalizations that the viewpoint character must keep the reader oriented by giving his interpretation of how things are going, what his options appear to be, and what he must try next. Thus internalizations—brief as they must be to be credible in an action scene—repeat the scene goal, show secondary goals as they may develop, and show the viewpoint character's idea of how things are going, and how he feels about it.

You might wish to study examples of published fiction involving scenes that are "all action." Dip into any of Jack Higgins's novels, for example, or most westerns. Paperback war novels also tend to stress action above everything else. It may surprise you as you read such authors to see how often the author has dipped into the character's mind for the purpose of keeping the reader oriented and understanding the scene's progression of events.

The *maneuver scene against an unseen opponent* usually takes place in action-adventure fiction. It's very similar to the all-action scene just described, the difference obviously being that there can't be the same kind of give-and-take because the opponent *is invisible*.

In such a scene—an outdoorsman maneuvering around a mountainside with the intent of blocking the escape of another man, for example—a sense of conflict is created by lengthening the internalizations and making the viewpoint character *consider alternatives and possible disasters* as he continually reevaluates the situation and second-guesses himself. Thus the viewpoint character might decide that his first step toward his goal of blocking his foe is to climb to a high vantage point where he can see everything. But on the way it occurs to him that, if he can see, he can also be seen—and possibly his invisible opponent is lying low at this moment, waiting for him to make just this predictable mistake. So the viewpoint character decides to change his momentary goal, and imagines where his opponent would most likely hide. As he imagines, it is almost as if we really could see the other character. And so our hero climbs a tree, but thinks he *might* have heard something down near the stream, sees how the opponent might logically have decided that the best way out was to wade the stream, so . . . and so on, and so on.

Such a scene is difficult to handle. It puts all the imagined stimuli inside the viewpoint character's thinking process, which is essentially a contradiction in terms of everything said up till now about stimulus and response. The contradiction can only be saved by showing physical stimuli like trees and the sound of the stream which trigger speculative thinking on the part of the viewpoint character, which he then analyzes in internalization, and acts upon *just as if he had really seen his opposition* instead of merely trying to anticipate his movements and outguess him.

MULTIPLE-AGENDA SCENES

When we turn to the matter of the *multiple-agenda scene*, we are about as far as we can get from the isolated scene of maneuver just described. Such multiple-agenda scenes should be avoided, as has been urged before. When you the author try to deal with two characters arguing about six or eight different issues all at once, the reader almost certainly is going to be confused about what is the bottom-line issue here, and what he is supposed to be worrying about. To put this another way, the multiple-agenda scene raises confusing *lists* of scene questions in the reader's mind.

There are, however, rare occasions when the hero simply *must* confront the entire board of directors, town council, or whatever. In such situations, you the author must maintain some kind of control by making the viewpoint character cling to his goal despite a variety of confusing countermaneuvers by all the other characters in opposition.

You must also, to keep things on track, make one of the antagonists stronger and more vocal than the others. By doing this, you will keep the main focus on the fight between him and the viewpoint character, even as others on the stage jump up and try to follow their individual, differing agendas.

Your plan for such a scene should first establish the viewpoint character's goal, then establish the opposition agenda of the major adversary you have selected, get that fight started, and then let the other secondary antagonists break in to interrupt the main fight at regular intervals. Throughout the interruptions, make sure that you keep the hero repeating his main goal *and experiencing all the side-conflict primarily as impediment to fighting out the main conflict*. You cannot allow him to get totally involved on some side issue. Both he and the major antagonist can in effect bang their gavels and demand to get back to the main point.

When you end such complicated scenes, it's all right for the viewpoint character evidently to win some of the minor side-skirmishes. The reader will worry if he does win some of them, because such developments will be seen as further motivation for more enemies to circle. The main scene conflict should be closed with a clear-cut disaster for the viewpoint character, as is usually the case.

In closing any discussion of scene-sequel structure variations or specialized situations calling for special handling techniques, I always feel compelled to point out yet again that stories are still imagined and planned in classic form. A writer could not handle any of the special devices mentioned in this chapter if she did not first clearly understand *what structural norm it was that she was departing from. Don't,* please, try any of these devices just because they sound neat. When a plot problem arises that demands one of them, you should be aware of it as a potential weapon in your arsenal. Until then, however, you are well advised to keep hands off and go on planning in the classic pattern and deviating as little as possible.

Review Appendix 5.
See Appendix 6.

CHAPTER 13

THE STRUCTURE
OF CHAPTERS

ALTHOUGH THE GENERAL PROBLEM can be dealt with rather quickly, questions about chapter length and construction occur so often at writers' conferences that brief attention should be given to the matter.

The first question usually asked is, *"How long should a chapter be?"* There is no single answer to this, unless you happen to be writing for a publisher whose tip sheet or editorial policy stipulates a standard chapter length. (A few romance publishers do.) Otherwise, the best answer one might give is "somewhere between ten and thirty manuscript pages — probably leaning toward the shorter end of this spectrum." But don't hold me to that answer.

I have written chapters as long as fifty manuscript pages — on my printer, close to 15,000 words. I have also written some as short as the following, which is *all* of chapter 25 of my novel *Dropshot.*

The orchestra was still playing in the ballroom, but the crowd had begun to thin sharply. It was 1 A.M. Sylvester strolled across the periphery of the large room, but kept going into the adjacent club where he had already noted L.K. Able perched on a stool at the far end of the bar.

Sylvester took the stool beside him and ordered Pernod.

"All is well," he told Able. "The transfer is completed."

"When will you hand it over to me?"

"There has been a change in instructions," Sylvester replied. He explained.

Able nodded. "I will verify the new orders."

"Of course. Now. About our friend."

"I watched Smith leave the villa after a very long interview. He proceeded to his car and from here to his cabin at a place called the Mary Mary. The lights were out. A power failure. They have them frequently in that section due to use of a gasoline generator for the few beach properties abutting the airport property on that side. It appeared he was turning in for the night, and I wanted to be sure to be back to meet you. Therefore I discontinued the surveillance and returned here."

"Was the woman with him tonight?"

"No."

"Strange. Is she here?"

"She was at the dance for a while with some of her new friends. Then she retired for the night. I saw her enter her room."

"Now. What about Hesser?"

"He retired for the night after Smith left him. The lights went out in his room almost at once. I feel sure he is sleeping."

"Excellent. You have done well."

Able paused, then asked, "Do you have further instructions for me at this point in time?"

"Your normal routine, I think. You will verify that, also, when you make your telephone call."

"Yes."

Sylvester downed the last of his Pernod. "I bid you goodnight." He slipped off the stool and walked out.

Clearly, unless your publisher has specified a desired length for his company's chapters, the length of a chapter is what you make it.

There simply is no ideal, model length for a chapter. The very division of novels into chapters is a wholly artificial convention that owes its existence in part to the needs of British publishers in the earliest days of the form: They published their stories in serials, like tabloid newspapers that came out once a week; so there had to be some kind of a breaking-off point every so often to signal an end to this week's installment—and hook the reader into buying next week's edition.

Still, you're writing a novel and you need some straight answers here. Much of what follows may not seem very "straight" to you, but the overriding principle can be made clearly enough.

The greatest danger to success of your story is that the reader will put it down during the reading and then not pick it up again. Where is the best place to put a book down? At the end of a chapter. Therefore the guiding philosophy about chapter construction must be this: Regardless of how long or short your chapters may be, *always end them at a point where the reader can't put the book down.*

You should try to have some general norm for chapter length in any given manuscript—an average chapter being fourteen typewritten pages, for example. *But if dramaturgy suggests a chapter of only one page here and there as the best way to keep your reader hooked, don't be afraid to do it.*

Why would a chapter of a page or even less sometimes be all right? Because the amount of information presented in some viewpoint, for example, might require no more than a page, but might be mandatory at a certain point in the novel. Or because some small (in physical size) scene ends with such a jarring disaster that you the author want to end the chapter with it even though you just ended the previous chapter a page earlier.

The best place to end a chapter is at the same place suggested as best for changing viewpoint: at the moment of disaster ending a scene.

The reasons are nearly the same as suggested for changing viewpoint at the disaster. The reader will turn the page eagerly to see what happens next—which makes the disaster the strongest reader-motivator there is. So you contrive your chapter plans so that a good disaster falls somewhere around the page number that you want (arbitrarily) to end a chapter. The reader is hit with the disaster—and you end the chapter. Your reader can't quit there—he has to start the next chapter to see what happens next.

The next-best place to end a chapter probably is right in the middle of the conflict. The goal is set, the fight starts, the reader is positively salivating with excitement—and you break the chapter. Your reader is mildly shocked by this break in the conflict, and turns the page, where he sees a new chapter heading and the conflict continuing immediately as if there had been no chapter break. Your reader *can't* quit under these circumstances!

Other good places to end chapters are obvious to you, I hope, after thinking about it a bit. You will lure your reader forward, more mildly than you would using one of the breaks mentioned above, but still strongly, if you end a chapter with your character stuck in his thought process of the sequel, thinking *there is no way out*. In a similar way, you can end the chapter at the decision point or the beginning of the new action (before conflict again starts) as the character resumes goal orientation and the reader can see what's next—and anticipate it with huge delight.

A chapter is not necessarily—and usually is *not*—composed of a single scene. If you analyze published novels, you will find three, four or more scenes linked inside the arbitrary fencings of chapter headings. You will also notice that the chapter endings are almost always at the point that will most strongly hook the reader into keeping on with the book and not putting it down at the end of the given chapter.

If a negative injunction might help, please note this well: You end chapters at places which will hook readers. *You do **not** devise your chapters to provide convenient blank spaces in between them for purposes of transition.*

This is such a common mistake in new writers that I wish there were a way to give it more emphasis. Time and time again, good novels are wrecked by poor chaptering—the author ending a chapter with a character going to sleep, for example, or putting in a chapter ending so that the next chapter can start some time later, the awkward transition having taken place between chapters. Chapters should always *link forward* in some way, and ending at nighty-night time, or using the space between chapters for author convenience in handling transitions, will turn the book into a series of clunky separate chapter units that stop so abruptly they practically scream at the reader to *"Stop here and put it down!"*

Examine your own chaptering practices carefully. As you near the place where something (usually the number of pages) tells you it's about time to end a chapter and start another, be sure that you ignore this niggling thought and keep going until you reach a point where you know the reader will not be able to stop. *Then* end the chapter, and don't worry if some chapters are short and others long, and the whole design doesn't seem "symmetrical" or something.

Readers don't care about symmetry, any more than they care about "smoothness of transitions." Readers want to be lured and hooked and dazzled and fascinated, and scene structure gives you all the weapons you need. End your chapters with the strongest hooks you can devise—usually scene-ending disasters—and the length of the chapters will take care of itself.

CHAPTER 14

THE SCENIC MASTER PLOT AND HOW TO WRITE ONE

IN PUTTING IT ALL TOGETHER in a finished novel, a writer uses every device at her disposal to capture the reader's attention, keep him intrigued without letup during the course of the story, and provide him with a smashing climax that will fully satisfy. As has been shown, understanding of scene and sequel structure, with their smaller component parts, gives the writer all the structural building blocks she needs to accomplish these tasks for the reader.

By varying the intensity of scenes now and then—having an occasional scene proceed from a very quiet goal to an extremely subtle disaster, for example—or using one of the other variations discussed earlier in this book, you can completely conceal the fact that you are working with the same basic building blocks over and over. At the same time, these components provide you with all the weaponry you need to keep the reader constantly moving forward with the story in a mounting tightness of suspense.

Knowing this, it's now time for us to take a look at how a writer might put everything together in a key pattern—a master plot, if you will—a plan for the content she will put in each part of her novel. The sample to be used is for a short suspense novel.

Every writer has in her mind some vague and generally unexamined idea of what a novel is *for her*. This mental prototype is different for every writer. Obviously, the prototype in the mind of a Jackie Collins is not very similar to the prototype in the mind of a Norman Mailer. Even two romance novelists selling to the same publishing house will have different master patterns in mind when they start to write; one may open with an immediate meeting of the heroine and her lover-to-be, for example, while the other novelist may tend to start by establishing the heroine and her career before having her meet a friend who will in turn lead her to the hero of the tale.

The more clear you can become about what *you* almost unconsciously assume as a model for your novel, the better you can manipulate scene structure to work in that very general pattern.

Now, my mental model for a novel is not yours—and my mental

picture of how a novel should be organized may change when I start planning my next book if it's a different type of story, a romantic tale as opposed to a suspense story, for example. Therefore it's supremely important for you to remember that a master plot is *not* a fill-in-the-blanks proposition, and it's not set in stone. It's nothing more than a very general description of the way *one* writer might write *one* novel—the kinds of events he would hope to have happen, and generally in what sequence.

How can this help you? By giving you some further insights into the kind of strategic planning that goes into one kind of book, I may help you find your way more clearly to ideas about how you should best use scenes and sequels to achieve certain effects and produce the kind of book that exists in your mind somewhere as an ideal, whether you previously realized it or not.

To use an analogy that won't hold up if you examine it *too* closely, let's say that your knowledge and practice of stimulus and response and the internal structure of scenes and sequels are a bit like knowledge of the fundamentals—blocking, tackling, how to hand the ball off, or how to catch it—for a football player. Your understanding of how to plan and present scenes for maximum effect, and how to link them with sequels, is like the skilled player's knowledge of the playbook. But one thing more needs to be added: In the case of the football player, it's a game plan—what plays will be selected in what circumstances, the general strategy to be employed during the course of the game under changing conditions, how field position will have an effect on the planned sequence of offensive plays, etc.

Your master plot is your game plan, your general idea of how you're going to put it all together for maximum effectiveness. It is completely flexible, and never *requires* you to have a certain kind of scene or sequel at any certain point. Further—I repeat this because it is so often misunderstood—it is *not* a fill-in-the-blanks that you should actually try to use. (Although some of my published novels can be seen to have many of the dramatic developments in them very closely patterned after the sample I'm to give you, even I have never produced a book that *exactly* follows this ideal sample, nor do I intend to.)

So if you study this brief master plot and try to do exactly what it describes, you'll be missing the whole point. All I'm trying to do is show you how one writer visualizes a short novel's dramatic development—give you a look into his mind as he puts scenes and sequels together in a long narrative.

Virtually everything in the first thirteen chapters of this book were based on the premise that good fiction is characterized by *movement*—meaning linear development from A through B to C in some kind of cause-and-effect relationship; such stories *get somewhere*, starting in one place, dramatically speaking, and ending up somewhere quite different. The master plot that follows may provide some insights into tactical planning intended to achieve this kind of linear story development and rising action.

In building a master plot or planning a blueprint for any novel, the writer's primary concern should be to keep the reader hooked and read-ing. The reader who abandons a novel at some point has not necessarily failed the novel; the novel probably has failed him. So a novelist works to keep the suspense high, whatever kind of book she is at work on.

Now, if you were to walk downtown tomorrow and see a street jug-gler *tossing up a single plate*, I don't think you would find it very interesting or suspenseful. If the juggler were to add a second plate, you might give him a glance. If he were to add a third, things might start to get interest-ing. Let the juggler get six plates in the air at once, and a crowd will have gathered. Why?

More plates = more things to worry about.

More things to worry about = greater suspense.

Greater suspense = more intense observer interest.

You the author must be a little like the juggler when you plan and write a story as long as a novel. We've already noted that you can't allow the story to be circular—characters endlessly arguing over exactly the same old ground; you can't even allow a scene's conflict segment to be circular. So what you have to do in devising a plan for a sequence of scenes is develop new twists and turns in the plot as the character tries different tacks in trying to reach his story goal. Each new twist—often meaning the logical but unanticipated disaster at the end of a scene—adds a new dimension to the central character's problem; it also often raises new ques-tions for the character—and the reader—to worry about. Thus "new plates" go up in the air.

In addition, your master plot probably will allow for additional plates to be tossed up, adding to reader tension, as secondary characters bring in their personal life stories and problems in trying to help the main viewpoint character or his primary opponent. Thus a novel made up of "a single story line" can get very complicated indeed, with a great many plates in the air for the reader to worry about.

Finally, while the paragraphs immediately above are completely true, they do not tell the whole story of the structure of most contempo-rary novels. Most novels today are not composed of a single story, intri-cately developed; they are made up of one major story line (complex as it may be) joined by two or six or eight lesser story lines or subplots (with their own related story questions) marching along with it in loose formation.

Each new subplot in a novel—each new subplot story question—is like another plate or pack of plates being put in the air by the street juggler. The more plates (up to some point), the more suspense and reader intensity. Thus your job as a novelist is more complex than earlier hinted in this book. Not only do you have to know how to build scenes and link them in various ways to build a single linear story line; you have to build *other* plots at the same time, then know how to juggle them and finally get all your plot plates down safely.

The following master plot attempts to give some ideas on how one writer might try to achieve all these objectives in one kind of story. It delineates in a general way the kind of dramatic "moves" an author might make at various points in the novel, and why.

We're going to assume that our goal is a short novel, perhaps 225 to 250 manuscript pages, 50,000 words or a bit more. Remember (again!) that *nothing about it is set in stone.* It merely shows you the kind of planning and thinking that might go into such a project.

A SCENIC MASTER PLOT

Prologue

This may or may not be used. If used, it is made up of a single scene, or two or three scene fragments. Its sole intention is to establish an immediate threat, aura of violence, sense of drama or romance, or whatever will intrigue and hook the reader. It should not exceed four or five manuscript pages, maximum. A dramatic "plate" or two go into the air: Who is involved here, what has happened, how bad will things become in the main body of the novel, who was that handsome man at the ball? This section is almost never told from the main character's viewpoint. The relationship between this prologue and the main story to come does not have to be at all apparent at once; it might be a sequence of events that do not obviously connect to chapter 1, which could mystify and further hook the reader. It might even be composed of two or three scene fragments which don't seem to relate to one another, thus setting up an aura of mystery. In terms of story time, it could take place moments before the opening of chapter 1, or far earlier. (In one of my suspense novels it takes place about eleven years before the present story opens in the first chapter.)

(Ordinarily the time span of the first three chapters should be very tight. Long time transitions early in a novel tend to slow it down, and your reader may not yet be hooked.)

Chapter One

Two or three scenes. Establishes the main character's viewpoint. This chapter is all in his viewpoint. A major change—perhaps learning of whatever happened in the prologue—perhaps something else entirely—alters the status quo and jars the main character off dead center. This chapter must start quickly, and hook the reader hard. That means starting at the beginning of a scene he has planned in the backstory, or being confronted by another character with that character's goal as the starter. For speed and a good reader hook, the opener can even start in the middle of an ongoing scene, or with an unforeseen disaster requiring immediate action.

Sample opening sentences:

> When he reached the apartment and kicked the door down, they had already killed the girl.

Or:

The letter arrived at noon, and nothing would ever be the same again.

Or:

"Like hell I'll take that case!" she said.
"You'll take it, or you're through here."

By the end of this chapter, the main character has formulated either the long-term major story goal or a short-term goal that will link into a few future chapters and make matters worse—or both. (At least two or three plates should go into the air.)

Chapter Two

Viewpoint of the major antagonist (hereafter called "the villain"). Two to four scenes show him or her as aggressive, dynamic, strongly motivated against the main character (hereafter called "the hero"), and already well into his first steps in his story-long quest or vendetta against the hero. Above all, this establishes the villain as powerful and ruthless. He has an immediate plan already under way. This goal is revealed or hinted at, thus putting up another story plate for the reader to worry about.

Chapter Three

Hero viewpoint. He deals with some aspect of the problem shown in chapter 1, and in two or three scenes comes into contact with two or three supporting characters, usually including the "best friend," a "minor antagonist," and the "romantic lead." Each of these characters has a small story of his own. Each in a small way represents another plate going into the air. This chapter usually has a scene or extended sequel which establishes some of the hero's background, and further shows his dedication to his main story goal. In the course of getting information from the secondary characters, or perhaps as a result of some new missile hurled from the hidden story by the villain or one of his aides, the hero painfully alters his original plans and comes up with a short-term goal (something that has to be accomplished to "clear the decks" before he can proceed on his major quest). The romantic question is usually planted here, too. The chapter usually ends at the end of a sequel, with the hero in motion toward his next big scene.

Chapter Four

This tricks the reader by going to other viewpoints—letting him worry awhile about the scene the hero was about to enter at the end of chapter 3. For the first time, some hours or even days may have elapsed between chapters, and there can be further time passage between the scenes in this chapter. We have several fairly short scenes from the viewpoint of one or more secondary characters while the hero is offstage somewhere. This chapter establishes secondary characters and their roles, and should intensify reader interest in their subsidiary story goals. If you have a major subplot to start, you start it here. One or more of the characters should talk about, and so characterize, the hero or the villain or the situation, or all three. Through this analysis, the reader should see higher stakes than earlier realized. This chapter should end with a scene disaster that is a startling new development obviously involving the hero's fate. The disaster puts up still another plate, this one perhaps short term, and raises a new "shocker question."

I am not going to explain further about the "shocker question" except to say that it is usually the stunning revelation of some allied problem, complication, or raising of the story stakes which was entirely unexpected by the cast prior to this point. The story needs a boost here, as assembly of the cast and introduction of secondary story lines has tended to slow things down a bit. The escalation of stakes, or whatever, jars the reader into renewed intensity of interest.

Chapter Five

Two to four scenes, all in the hero's viewpoint, in which he struggles with the shocker question disaster and helps the secondary character or characters to solve it. The moment he has accomplished this, however, he must return to his own short-term quest, as alluded to (at least) in chapter 1. This should be seen by the author as a *three-chapter quest, investigation or trip*; it will raise a new subplot story question—another plate—which will come down in chapter 8. The hero, or circumstances, may set a short-term ticking clock here. "I'm going to have the answer to this by Saturday night, or else." The time span between this point and chapter 8 must be brief—perhaps hours, more likely a day or two.

Chapter Six

Four scenes. Two or three in the viewpoint of the romantic lead as she pursues her own subplot goal, or tries to help the hero (now offstage) in some way. Often a sequel here defines her background and personality. A function of this chapter may also be to introduce a "red herring" or two—a false clue, bad lead or character who seems suspicious but may actually be innocent. One scene in this chapter might well be villain viewpoint as he gets wind of the romantic lead's plan of action, or the hero's three-chapter quest, and begins to countermove. One effect of this chapter on the reader, psychologically, is to tantalize him, drawing out the time before he can read about the hero's exciting short-term quest.

Chapter Seven

Hero viewpoint. He is embroiled in his three-chapter quest. Three scenes: one leading him nearer a confrontation with the villain, the second momentarily delaying him or complicating his situation, the third bringing him into direct confrontation with the villain or a minion. This is an *action sequence*—preferably physical: a car chase, a face-to-face confrontation with violent words and emotions, perhaps even an attack on the hero's life. This is the first really big peak in the book. The end of the chapter is at a new disaster which will allow no time for sequel, or at some turning point in the middle of the ongoing scene. This chapter hooks instantly into the next.

Chapter Eight

Chapter 7's climactic scene continues. It is still the hero's point of view. The villain pulls some unexpected and potentially catastrophic trick to get the upper hand, or seem to, and the hero teeters on the edge of a disaster that would not only end his three-chapter quest with total defeat, but possibly end his story entirely. The chapter-opening scene continuation furnishes this disaster, and then there may or may not be time for a sequel, but if there is one, it should be brief. In the next scene, the hero narrowly wins or escapes, but does not fully realize his three-chapter quest goal. This is his disaster, often shown in a chapter-ending sequel in which the romantic lead and/or best friend come to help him lick his wounds. There can be a hint of stronger romantic attraction here, reemphasizing the ongoing romantic subplot question. Maybe she hints of some complication to the possibility of a relationship, which would toss another plate in the air.

Chapter Nine

Mostly the villain's viewpoint. First a sequel showing his reaction-feeling and thoughts that he did not attain his ends in chapter 8, and so also in his own way experienced a disaster. Thus set back, he lays new plans, but often reestablishes his own villainy by doing something terrible to someone else — perhaps a henchman he can blame for the chapter 8 debacle as he sees it. If you are developing a major subplot, and started it by establishing the secondary character in chapter 4, this is an excellent place to return to that character's viewpoint and move his story line along to its next logical dropping-off point — a disaster, we hope. At the end of this chapter, the villain is just moving into a new scene with a goal which may or may not be stated. In either case, it raises another villain plot question — another plate.

Chapter Ten

Three to five scenes and sequels, most in hero viewpoint, possibly one in romantic lead viewpoint. The hero reevaluates, heals up, collects new information, reexamines everything that has happened and his motives. (The author asks herself here: "Why doesn't he just resign from this story, if it's this hard?" She then has the character, in effect, ask himself the same thing, and give an answer about his motivation.) The main story goal is restated here, perhaps in different terms in light of bad things that have happened here, near the midpoint of the book. The romantic subplot question usually becomes much stronger here, sometimes with a first sexual encounter (postcoital sequel is a good time for a dialogue sequel to review the plot and consider plans), other times without sex and even with further complications in the romance which make it appear doomed. At any rate, the romantic plot questions—will they end up together?—*must not* be answered until much, much later. At the end of this chapter, the hero is committed anew, and moving back toward new action.

(A note on general strategy here: Novels often start well and busily because there is so much to set up and get moving. Just as often, they end with a fine rush of excitement as "all the plates come tumbling down." It's in the boggy middle where so many novels fail. For that reason, this sample master plot format injects a four-chapter "mini-novel" in the middle of the book, a story-within-a-story, designed to be very fast-paced, related to the central story question but often with side issues involved, and a ticking clock whenever possible. This mini-novel is designed to entrance the reader in very fast-moving action and development for four chapters, thus getting the story to the point where plates can start coming down and the story can begin to move toward its climax.)

Chapter Eleven

Two to five scenes, all in hero viewpoint. He sets out on the course of action he decided in chapter 10, and immediately is thwarted, or runs into, the course of action plotted by the villain. This must be a strong, fast-moving, action-oriented sequence of events. Each scene shows the hero's maneuver thwarted in disaster, with little time for a thought-out sequel. There may be "contact scenes" here—scenes butting directly into other scenes with no sequel at all. This may involve a chase, a capture, a cornering, or a very strong turn of events that puts the hero into desperate, time-restricted action. Often there can be another ticking clock. The chapter ends with a strong, immediate action hook at the end of a scene.

Chapter Twelve

Continues chapter 11 with little or no time gap between them. The villain clearly gets the upper hand. If we did not know the villain's motives earlier, or his plan, we see them now. A small part of the general story mystery is solved, but in action that makes it unlikely the hero will live to use it. At the end of the third scene in this chapter—all in hero viewpoint again—there is an even more terrible scene-ending disaster as the hero's "last ploy" fails—and he faces ultimate ruin.

Chapter Thirteen

To tantalize the reader, this chapter turns to the viewpoint(s) of the romantic lead or the best friend or others. It may be that one scene here shows the romantic lead trying to solve whatever subplot problem she sees as standing between her and the hero, but the disaster ending this scene is some knowledge of the hero's present plight, or revelation to her of where he went, what he was going to try to do. She and/or the best friend rush to try to help, but the ticking clock tells the reader that they will be too late. (The cavalry never comes to the rescue! The hero will have to get out of the mini-novel on his own.)

An alternative here, if a major subplot has been developing, is a lengthy return to that character's viewpoint for story review and analysis, and possibly the injection of considerable backstory. (This is the sort of move that was being made by the author in Appendix 5.)

Chapter Fourteen

One or two big action scenes climax and bring to a close the mini-novel. The hero momentarily survives and gains some ground, but the villain "gets away" to fight again. This chapter often ends in a sequel—perhaps with the friends who arrived too late to help—in which the hero sees that new information gained through the mini-novel now make somewhat clear his future course of action. Sometimes here he will have new difficulty with the romantic lead, or his best friend may even turn on him with suspicion. The hero is near his wits' end and must start his final novel game plan, planting still another story question. If a clock has not been set ticking before, it is started here—the time or goal that will end the story clearly in view, and time running out.

Chapter Fifteen

Three to six scenes, all in viewpoints other than the hero. They see the big picture, and make new moves. The romantic lead is in despair. The villain plans his new strategy in sequel to what he (again) experienced as a disaster, this time in the mini-novel. If there has been a red herring character or major subplot, this chapter clears the red herring or brings the subplot quite near its conclusion. (It is mandatory to start bringing down some plates this early, because the novel is beginning to end.) Very often, the romantic lead—either in a disaster set up in a scene where she tried to be of further help, or as a result of a shot from the hidden story by the scheming villain—is thrown into grave peril here. This puts up another short-term worry-plate about her safety.

Chapter Sixteen

About four scenes, all hero viewpoint, a series of scenes in which he tries repeatedly to "crack the case," and is thwarted each time. If there has still been some lack of clarity about how the Prologue related to this story, the connection must by now be made completely clear. The present plot clock is ticking. The hero finds the villain and meets him again more or less on his (the hero's) terms this time. But the tables are turned at the end of scene three, and some violence occurs. Often a villain's henchman or friend of the hero come to a bad end here. The hero learns of the romantic lead's plight and rushes to help. This makes an immediate hook at the end of the chapter.

Chapter Seventeen

Three scenes, possibly four, in various viewpoints including the villain's. The romantic lead is freed, or that kind of subplot question answered, but at the cost of putting the hero on weaker ground. The romantic lead is left disillusioned and thinking the love story is over. At the end of the last scene, the hero and villain are closing in on one another, or perhaps are already face-to-face on a rooftop, in a courtroom, on the side of a mountain, in the drawing room. The showdown is *now*.

Chapter Eighteen

The ultimate confrontation takes place in one long, exciting, extended scene. If there has been a backstory or hidden story of significance, it now comes out and all those plates come down. Most secondary plot line questions are answered, and the only ones left are about this showdown . . . and the romance which now seems doomed. The villain, in the scene closing this chapter, plays his last, shocking trump card, and it is ultimate disaster for the hero.

Chapter Nineteen

Probably two scenes. In the first, the villain, with the upper hand, may offer the hero a way out of his dilemma if he will do something immoral, unethical or illegal. This poses a moral dilemma for the hero, who must choose fast between the good (by the reader's definition) decision—and lose everything, perhaps including his own life—or select the bad course of action, and be given some sort of break by the powerful villain. The hero chooses sacrificially, in most cases, reopening the fight because this ultimate test has shown him to be a person who will not go back on certain basic principles fundamental to his self-concept. The biggest fight, chase, struggle, argument, or maneuvering of all take place here, with the author pulling out every stop and "topping" all that has gone before in terms of suspense, terror and possibly violence. At the end, the hero's scene, unlike all others in the book preceding this one—*ends well*. In this single case, he somehow wins. But he is often left in sequel, wondering something like "What did it all mean?" *or* "Was it worth it?" This "downside" questioning, right after an apparent victory over the villain, raises a final thematic question for the reader to worry about as a hook into the last chapter. (He also has the romantic story question still up in the air.)

Chapter Twenty

Worry about the romantic story question lures the reader into the final chapter, where the author usually uses two to three short scenes, invariably in the viewpoint of the main character, to tie up loose plot threads. Secondary characters who have played fairly big roles often must be trotted onstage in the last chapter to show their feelings and condition at the end of the book—providing what psychologists would term "closure." The meaning of everything that has happened often comes somewhat clearer here. The romantic subplot question is finally answered at the very end of a scene between the hero and the romantic lead, sometimes with the best friend as a witness or commentator. The answer to the romantic question, like the answer to the main question in the entire book, must be *addressed*, but the answer may be something less than perfect. ("Perhaps we'll never know why he tried to kidnap the president." *Or:* "Will I marry you? I don't know yet, Frank. I really don't. But we can see. . . ." How clearly, happily and finally these last questions are answered will depend on the kind of closing feeling the author wishes to leave with the reader. An ending that is too neat and happy in all regards may be experienced by the reader as a cheap trick.) At any rate, the closing usually comes in a scene, often in the middle of one, so that there is some sense of the story "going on after the book is closed."

Having read through this scenario, you may begin to see how its author wanted certain kinds of things to happen in certain parts of the novel; he had a general idea of strategy—ideas of the kind of dramatic moves to make at certain points—and so his master plot or story blueprint set up a sequence of scenes and sequels generally intended to accomplish his ends.

I hope you will try to work on your own "master plot." Far from being a straitjacket, it can be a dynamic, ongoing, developing manifestation of your growing understanding of scene and structure, and how they are the building blocks of success.

APPENDICES

The following appendix entries are excerpts from published fiction which illustrate one or more points developed in the text. Each is followd by a brief analytical commentary which is meant to be more suggestive than exhaustive.

Chapter-ending notes refer the reader to various exhibits as appropriate. To get the most from each appendix exhibit, it would be best to read each carefully at the instruction point suggested in the text, then mark it up marginally as seems appropriate. Only after doing this analytical work on her own should the student read the commentary that follows it. By comparing your observations with the author's, you can perhaps further clarify your thinking and "cement" your understanding of a principle by seeing it in action.

Because many of the techniques illustrated in the excerpts are interrelated, a rereading of all of them is recommended after all of the chapters have been studied.

APPENDIX 1

HOW TO START YOUR STORY AND HOW TO END IT

This appendix is made up of two separate excerpts from published fiction. Commentary on each excerpt can be found following the excerpt.

EXCERPT 1

This is the opening of chapter 1 of *The Savage Day*, by Jack Higgins. Holt, Rinehart & Winston, © 1972 by Jack Higgins.

1	1
2	EXECUTION DAY
3	They were getting ready to shoot somebody in the inner
4	courtyard, which meant it was Monday because Monday was exe-
5	cution day.
6	Although my own cell was on the other side of the building,
7	I recognized the signs: a disturbance from those cells from which
8	some prisoners could actually witness the whole proceedings and
9	then the drums rolling. The commandant liked that.
10	There was silence, a shouted command, a volley of rifle fire.
11	After a while, the drums started again, a steady beat accompany-
12	ing the cortege as the dead man was wheeled away, for the com-
13	mandant liked to preserve the niceties, even on Skarthos, one of
14	the most unlovely places I have visited in my life. A bare rock in
15	the Aegean with an old Turkish fort on top of it containing three
16	thousand political detainees, four hundred troops to guard them,
17	and me.
18	I'd had a month of it, which was exactly four weeks too long,
19	and the situation wasn't improved by the knowledge that some of
20	the others had spent up to two years there without any kind of
21	trial. A prisoner told me during exercise one day that the name
22	of the place was derived from some classical Greek root meaning
23	barren which didn't surprise me in the slightest.

24   Through the bars of my cell you could see the mainland, a
25   smudge on the horizon in the heat haze. Occasionally, there was
26   a ship, but too far away to be interesting, for the Greek Navy
27   ensured that most craft gave the place a wide berth. If I craned
28   my head to the left when I peered out there was rock, thorn
29   bushes to the right. Otherwise, there was nothing to see and noth-
30   ing to do except lie on the straw mattress on the floor which was
31   exactly what I was doing on that May morning when everything
32   changed.

Commentary

Line 3. (The first line of the excerpt) Speak of starting swiftly and not trusting the reader to be patient! The first seven words of the novel establish action already in progress — and dynamic, dangerous, violent action at that.

Line 6. The phrase "my own cell" establishes that the story is to be told from the viewpoint of a first-person narrator. Again, the professional writer does not wait to establish such things.

Lines 10-17. Note the use of sense-appealing concrete details. Nothing abstract here: "shouted" command, "volley of rifle fire," the "steady beat" of the drum. A few carefully selected words set up the harsh story world in a strong physical sense. And by the end of the short paragraph we know *where* the setting is, *what* it is called, *how* it is set up, and *how* the viewpoint narrator fits in.

Lines 18-21. We learn how long the narrator has been there, and the fact that some prisoners wait years for a trial. Although there has been no sign of an opening change to jar the story into forward motion, even the situation *prior to* the change is threatening in the extreme.

Lines 31-32. ". . . when everything *changed*." (Italics supplied here.)

This excerpt gives a professional novelist a thrill of delight. It seems perfect. It starts with a colorful situation that is already ghastly for the central character, who is introduced at once. Threat is established in the opening lines. Then a change comes — and the story must start moving forward at once.

EXCERPT 2

The opening of chapter 1 of *Dropshot*, by Jack M. Bickham. Tor Books, © 1990 by Jack M. Bickham.

1   ONE
2   Al Hesser's letter arrived early on a beautiful October day in
3   Dallas, the kind of day that makes you forgive the ugly sky-anvil
4   days of spring and the endless dusty furnace of summer: a day
5   perfectly cobalt clear, with the temperature at seventy and only

6 | the faintest breeze out of the south. Only a crazy man could fail
7 | to rejoice on such a day.
8 | Unfortunately, it was the autumn I was pretty crazy.

Commentary

I hope the reader will forgive me for using some excerpts from my own published work. It's done not out of a desire for ego-gratification, but as a convenience: I know my own work, and can recall my intentions at the time I produced it; thus it's to be hoped that my commentary will make sense.

Lines 2-3. The change is specified at once, with no delay of any kind: the arrival of a letter. The time and place of opening are also set up in the first dozen words.

Lines 3-6. Concrete, physical details are designed to establish the setting not in the abstract, but at the gut level of physical sensing.

Line 8. A second "hook" for the reader. (*"What does he mean, he's crazy? Why is he crazy?"*) A change—in the form of a letter—has already come, although we don't know its contents as yet. But as in the Higgins excerpt previously examined, the change hits a character already in an abnormal, threatened state.

The moral (again): Stories start with change. And in today's world they do not start subtly or slowly.

APPENDIX 2

STRUCTURE IN MICROCOSM: CAUSE AND EFFECT

This appendix contains one excerpt. Commentary follows it. Excerpt from chapter 18 of *The Dark Wind*, by Tony Hillerman. Harper & Row, © 1982 by Tony Hillerman. In this excerpt, officer Jim Chee questions a character named Cowboy Dashee. Another character named Pauling listens in silence.

1	"What's new?" Chee asked.
2	"You talked to your office this morning?"
3	"No," Chee said.
4	"You haven't heard about finding the car, or turning up the
5	necklace?"
6	"Necklace?"
7	"From the Burnt Water burglary. Big squash blossom job.
8	Girl over at Mexican Water pawned it."
9	"Where'd she get it?"
10	"Who else?" Cowboy said. "Joseph Musket. Old Ironfingers
11	playing Romeo." Cowboy turned to Miss Pauling. "Shop talk," he
12	said. "Mr. Chee and I have been worrying about this burglary
13	and now a piece of the loot finally turned up."
14	"When?" Chee asked. "How'd it happen?"
15	"She just pawned it yesterday," Cowboy said. "Said she met
16	this guy at a squaw dance over there somewhere, and he wanted
17	to . . ." Cowboy flushed slightly, glanced at Miss Pauling. "Any-
18	way, he got romantic and he gave her the necklace."
19	"And it was Ironfingers."
20	"That's what she said his name was." Cowboy grinned at
21	Chee. "I notice with intense surprise that you're not interested in
22	the car."
23	"You said you found it?"
24	"That's right," Cowboy said. "Just followed a sort of hunch I
25	had. Followed up an arroyo out there and believe it or not, there
26	it was, hidden up under some bushes."

27	"Good for you," Chee said.
28	"I'll tell you what's good for me," Cowboy said. "I jimmied
29	my way into it through the vent on the right front window, pried
30	it right open."
31	"That's the best way to get in," Chee said.
32	"I thought you'd say that," Cowboy said.

Commentary

This dialogue excerpt derives its logical, straightforward movement from careful observation of stimulus and response.

Line 1. Chee provides a stimulus with a direct question.

Line 2. Cowboy does not respond directly, but sends a counter-stimulus question, to which Chee responds immediately in the next line.

Lines 3-10. Stimulus-response questions and answers link tightly as Chee seeks and receives additional information.

Lines 11-13. Cowboy momentarily gets off the straight stimulus-and-response pattern by acting upon some internalization which the reader cannot know since the reader is not in Cowboy's viewpoint.

Line 14. Chee immediately brings Cowboy back by resuming stimulus-questioning.

Line 27. For the first time, Chee does not send a direct stimulus in his spoken words.

Line 28. Cowboy makes his next statement responsive by repeating Chee's words "good for." Thus, although the content of Chee's last remark was not an obvious stimulus, the author makes it work as a stimulus in the way it is worded — and by showing how Cowboy picks up on the words and repeats them in a different context.

APPENDIX 3

STRUCTURE IN LARGER ELEMENTS: THE SCENE

This appendix contains one excerpt. Commentary follows it.

Excerpt is from chapter 2 of *Tiebreaker*, by Jack M. Bickham. Tor Books, © 1989 by Jack M. Bickham. In this excerpt, the novel's central viewpoint character, Brad Smith, has just returned to his condominium late at night to find an intruder inside. Smith slips in, armed, and finds that the intruder is a longtime associate from his CIA days, Collie Davis.

1 He grinned at me and my weapon. "This is great. This is
2 really dramatic."
3 He was tall but not as lanky as I remembered him from our
4 last meeting almost five years previously, wearing Levi's and a
5 madras shirt and camp loafers. In those days he had looked like
6 a kid, but now he had lost a little of his sandy hair, and his face
7 had been roughened by unacceptable losses. Under some circum-
8 stances I might have been happy to see him again.
9 "Where did you park?" he asked improbably.
10 I put the revolver on the TV set with an angry thunk. "You
11 were really stupid to come in here this way, you know."
12 "If you had parked in front, or opened your garage door, I
13 would have heard you and turned on more lights so you wouldn't
14 get all paranoid."
15 "I might have shot your head off."
16 "Are you kidding me? I've seen you shoot."
17 "What do you want, Collie?"
18 He uncoiled from my chair. "You look a little strung out."
19 "What do you *want*, Collie?"
20 Collie Davis turned the TV off and sat down again, but this
21 time on the couch, leaving me my chair. "It was really pretty im-
22 portant to see you as soon as possible, but not in the public eye."
23 So he had driven into the fringes of the neighborhood,
24 walked up the alley, picked the lock on one of my doors, and come
25 in like a second-rate burglar. It didn't strike me as all that smart.

26 | But there had always been things about the Company that didn't
27 | make a lot of sense to me, so I chose not to argue about it.
28 | I repeated, "What do you want, Collie?"
29 | "We've got a little contract job."
30 | "I'm not interested in going to Norman or someplace and
31 | interviewing college candidates."
32 | "How would you feel about Belgrade?"
33 | "What state is that in?"
34 | "Funny. Shall I start at the beginning?"
35 | "You can start," I told him, "by getting out of here."
36 | "We need a tennis player. Tennis journalist."
37 | "What for?"
38 | "Go to Belgrade for their new tournament, do some journal-
39 | ism, play in the celebrity matches, handle something routine for
40 | us on the side."
41 | "The Belgrade International is in less than two weeks."
42 | "Right."
43 | "That doesn't give me or anyone else a lot of time."
44 | "It gives enough."
45 | "Why me?"
46 | "You fit the job description. There aren't many who do."
47 | "Get Ted Sherman," I said, naming another former tennis
48 | pro who, like me, had done some scut work for them in earlier
49 | years while earning his real money on the players' circuit.
50 | "We prefer you. You're more reliable and you've had more
51 | training." He paused to light a cigarette. "Besides, he's in the
52 | hospital with back trouble."
53 | "So I'm the best man for the job because I'm the only man?"
54 | He ignored that. "Do you know Danisa Lechova?"
55 | "The Yugoslav singles player? Sure. I know who she is. We've
56 | never met."
57 | "She's 21 now," Collie told me unnecessarily, "and most peo-
58 | ple think she'll be the number one women's player in the world
59 | by next year this time. They've brought her along very slowly,
60 | evidently guarding against the kind of burnout that seems to hit
61 | a lot of the potentially great female players just as they start to
62 | win big. But many people think she'll be better than Navratilova,
63 | Mandlikova or Graf inside another year. May already be."
64 | I had seen Lechova play on television, and had been im-
65 | pressed. She was tall, slender, blond, beautiful, and absolutely un-
66 | flappable, combining the cool of a Chrissie with the dynamite
67 | attack of a Martina. "She's great," I conceded. "So what?"
68 | "So she didn't play in the Wimbledon that just finished."
69 | "Strained knee, I heard."
70 | "Wrong."
71 | "What's right, then?"
72 | "The Yugoslav government kept her out. Now they've set up
73 | this whole invitational tourney in Belgrade to showcase her and

74 her sister."

75   "Are you telling me she wasn't injured—that they kept her
76 from traveling to England for the biggest tournament in the
77 world?"

78   "Precisely. They pulled her passport. Her sister Hannah's,
79 too. They can't leave Yugoslavia."

80   "Jesus Christ. Why?"

81   "Who knows for sure?"

82   "You do."

83   "No. Really."

84   "I think you're lying."

85   He shrugged. "The point is, she's had enough of it. She wants
86 to defect to the U.S."

87   "Why doesn't she just wait until the U.S. Open in September
88 and walk out of the locker room and ask for asylum? Surely her
89 passport thing will be cleared up by then."

90   "Don't bet on it."

91   I thought about it. "Collie, what are you not telling me?"

92   "Nothing," he said, lying smoothly enough.

93   "There may be a lot of people over there who would like to
94 come to the West," I pressed. "Why is she of such interest to us?
95 She may be great, but she's still just a tennis player."

96   Collie's jaw set. "There are good reasons."

97   "Want to name one?"

98   "There's no need for you to know."

99   I sighed. Somehow I had known he would say that. They
100 were very dramatic sometimes, these guys. "All right, then," I
101 said. "Danisa Lechova wants out, you think you can get her out
102 during the tournament over there, and I can help. How?"

103   "All you have to do is go over there, play in the celebrity, write
104 some copy, interview her a couple of times, and facilitate commu-
105 nication between her and the people who will do the work."

106   "A go-between."

107   "Yes."

108   "Is it that hard for her to talk to people?"

109   "We can't risk their seeing her talking direct to our people
110 on the scene."

111   "They watch her that closely?"

112   "They keep a pretty close eye on her, yes."

113   " 'They' being the UDBA?"

114   He looked a lot more uncomfortable. "And possibly the
115 KGB."

116   "The Jugs have never let the Russians meddle in their inter-
117 nal affairs. And you're telling me the UDBA and the KGB are
118 *cooperating* in watching Danisa Lechova?"

119   "It's an unusual case, Brad," he said lamely.

120   "I think you better tell me what's so special about this girl."

121   "I've told you as much as I need to. Besides, your part is

122 | relatively straightforward."
123 | "Right. The last time one of you gave me that line, I almost
124 | got my kneecaps crushed."
125 | "This is different. This is easy."
126 | "Just dodge the UDBA and the KGB. Right."
127 | "Well, there's also a minor problem with her coach."
128 | "Fjbk? Is Fjbk still coaching her?"
129 | "Yes. Miloslav Fjbk. Serb. Not a bad player once. Great coach.
130 | You know, I'm sure, about the work he did with Lendl a few years
131 | back; Lendl went to him. Fjbk sees Lechova as his greatest pro-
132 | duction as a coach. Also, although he's an old fart—over 40—it
133 | appears he's interested in a lot more than the lovely Danisa's back-
134 | hand."
135 | I let the old fart comment pass. "So the man who makes
136 | contact with her will have a jealous lover glowering nearby."
137 | "He's not her lover. We're told she isn't even aware of his
138 | crush. He's . . . circumspect. But our informants say he watches
139 | her like a sheepdog, and goes crazy if she so much as smiles at a
140 | young man her own age."
141 | "Well, that's good, then," I said. "Fjbk shouldn't worry about
142 | me. I'm almost as old a fart as he is."
143 | Collie missed my irony. "You'll go, then." He stabbed his ciga-
144 | rette into the ashtray.
145 | "I don't know. This all sounds fishy as hell to me."
146 | He gave me his sincere, let's-be-honest look, which he did
147 | rather well. "Brad, would we lie to you?"
148 | "Yes."
149 | "It's routine."
150 | "I may not be very smart, Collie, but I've done enough for
151 | you guys to know that these last-minute assignments are never
152 | quite routine."
153 | "Well, we realize that it's inconvenient for you. So I'm author-
154 | ized to offer more than the usual $160 a day per diem."
155 | My suspicions deepened, but only enough to resemble the
156 | Grand Canyon. "How much more?"
157 | "Whatever you think is fair," he told me with opaque eyes.
158 | "And it's routine," I said sarcastically. "Right."
159 | "The highest authority wants her out of there as soon as pos-
160 | sible, and the Yugoslav International gives us our chance. You're
161 | the only man who can get close enough to her to work well as our
162 | go-between. You can name your own contract price on this one.
163 | You can make a small fortune."
164 | I walked to the door. "Okay. That's it. Out."
165 | He looked startled. "What did I say?"
166 | "You son of a bitch. I never did *anything* for you people for
167 | the money."
168 | "I didn't mean to imply—"
169 | "I'm not rich," I cut in, really steamed, "but I'm getting

170 | along. If you want a mercenary, go find one of your turncoats, out
171 | making a mint of taxpayer money on the college lecture circuit,
172 | telling the kids how awful the CIA is. Tell one of *them* to name
173 | their own price. They'll probably be willing to sell you their loyalty
174 | again for a week or ten days, if the price is high enough."
175 | "Calm down, Brad. My God."
176 | "You calm down, Collie. On your way out of here."
177 | "I was just trying to show you that it's a vital assignment."
178 | I looked at him and took a few deep breaths. The fatigue and
179 | disappointment of the match had frayed my temper. I had been
180 | too sensitive, perhaps.
181 | I said, "If I do it, it won't be for the money."
182 | "Fine."
183 | "I'll take per diem. Nothing more."
184 | His lips quirked. "How noble. You and Ollie North, right?"
185 | "Screw you."
186 | Collie yawned.
187 | I told him, "And I might not do it anyway."
188 | He grinned, irritatingly confident again. "We'll provide you
189 | with a printout of background information on these people and
190 | precisely what we want done, and how we want you to do it."
191 | "When do I get that?"
192 | "You can get it tomorrow, but you'll have to go down to the
193 | Federal Building in downtown Dallas and meet me there to read
194 | it. The orders say none of it leaves the office."
195 | "You break in here in the middle of the night to avoid our
196 | being seen together, and then I'm supposed to waltz into the Fed-
197 | eral Building? In broad daylight?"
198 | He looked blank. "Who would recognize you?"
199 | "Thanks!"
200 | "So what do you say? Are you onboard for this one?"
201 | "I just have a few thousand questions to clear up first. How
202 | do I get an invitation to play in the celebrity over there?"
203 | "We can take care of that."
204 | "I don't have an assignment. It's not believable that a free-
205 | lance tennis writer flies clear the hell and gone to Belgrade to
206 | cover a new tournament on speculation."
207 | "Assignments from one or two of the big tennis magazines
208 | can be arranged."
209 | "And I'm supposed to go over there, contact Danisa Lechova,
210 | then pass messages back and forth between her and the people
211 | who will actually get her out."
212 | "Right. Simple."
213 | I knew *that* was a lie. I asked him more questions. He was
214 | evasive. The printouts, he said, would tell me all I needed to know.
215 | There was far too much here that I didn't know. That was
216 | one of the reasons I was interested. It was clear that the Company
217 | really wanted this girl . . . was ready to mount an extraordinary

218 effort to get her out promptly. I was very curious why. And I had
219 helped before on no more basis than realization that *somebody*
220 thought it was important.
221   Still, I kept probing and he kept dodging. We maneuvered
222 for quite a long time. Finally it became clear that I was going to
223 accept or reject this job on the basis of vastly incomplete informa-
224 tion. I gave up trying.
225   "Okay," I said wearily.
226   "So you're onboard," Collie said with satisfaction, trying to
227 close like an insurance salesman.
228   "I'll read the printouts."
229   "Which means you're onboard."
230   "Which means I'll read the printouts."
231   "Close enough."
232   "When and where in the Federal Building?"
233   "Tomorrow. Two o'clock. I'll meet you at the testing office."
234 He got up to leave. It was almost 3 A.M.
235   "Incidentally," I told him at the back door, "about our Ted
236 Sherman. Who can't take this assignment because he's in the hos-
237 pital?"
238   "Right. Back trouble."
239   "I heard," I told him, "that he went someplace for you people
240 a few months ago, and got his cover blown by some people who
241 weren't as gentlemanly as we try to be. I heard they stuck an
242 anode up his penis and talked to him a long time with the high
243 voltage on. I heard he's in the hospital because he now lacks a lot
244 of physical equipment that most men value very highly, and it's
245 going to take the shrinks a long time with him after the urologists
246 and plastic surgeons get done."
247   "God!" Collie said. "Where did you ever hear crap like that?
248 That's ridiculous! Totally untrue. *Totally.*"
249   "Really?"
250   "Absolutely!" He looked sincerely shocked.
251   Good liar, Collie.

Commentary

Lines 1-16. This opening dialogue exchange functions primarily to show
Smith's emotional reaction to the shock of finding his old associate hiding
in his condominium in the middle of the night. It also describes Davis a
bit, and establishes the kind of sarcastic, sardonic relationship the two men
have. Although they are in action here, however, a scene cannot be said
to have started because neither man has yet stated a goal.

Line 17. Although presumably Davis had some goal for this meeting
first—he having initiated it—it is the viewpoint character, Smith, who
states a goal first: He wants to know what Collie Davis wants from him.
(*Scene question:* Will Smith learn what Davis wants?)

Lines 20-22. Davis does not respond directly to Smith's question. The reader will experience such nonresponsive behavior as conflictful.

Lines 23-27. Smith responds first in an internalization to Davis's uninformative reply. In this internalization, he decides to press his goal.

Line 28. Smith repeats his goal.

Line 29. Davis gives a direct response to the stimulus-question, but is vague. (If he were to blurt out everything at once, there would be no scene tension and he would make a multiple-page speech. For drama, Smith must drag the information out of him, bit by bit.)

Lines 38-39. Davis becomes more specific.

Line 45. Now having some information, Smith changes the ground on which the scene is being fought. He is still seeking information on Davis's mission here, but now asks "Why me?"

Line 46. Davis replies directly.

Lines 47-48. Smith begins trying to get out of taking the job, while fishing for further details.

Line 54. Davis begins bringing out more information, but in the form of a question.

Lines 80-84. Very tightly woven moment-by-moment stimulus-response dialogue.

Lines 85-86. Davis further defines his mission, what he wants.

Line 91. A brief internalization is hinted at but not presented. Smith shifts ground again, voicing a new suspicion.

Line 120. Smith is still pressing for what he believes Davis is holding back from him.

Line 127. Davis gives more information—all bad news.

Lines 146-152. Smith knows a lot by now, but his suspicions have only deepened. He has made good progress from the start of the scene, where he merely wanted to know in general what Davis wanted. But many new questions have arisen in his mind.

Lines 153-186. Always be alert for the opportunity to introduce new angles in the conflict. Here Davis's casual mention of extra pay for the assignment angers Smith, who protests that he is not a mercenary. (Of course this functions to characterize Smith, as well as to complicate the conflict.)

Lines 209-211. Smith repeats what he has come to know, to review for the reader.

Line 212. Davis agrees totally.

Lines 213-220. Smith's internalization to show what he is thinking in response to the stimulus of Davis's apparent lie.

Lines 221-224. Although it's a rule that one never should summarize in a scene, here is summary! Why? Because the argument has gotten to the brink of repetitiveness, and to string it out further might lose the reader's attention. However, since all the needed development has already been done, and this should be a very difficult decision for Smith, a bit of summary is inserted to indicate to the reader that Smith did not get to a decision in the time span of a few minutes.

Line 225. Smith agrees to Davis's unstated but clearly implied scene goal, to get him on board.

Line 232. Smith needs a bit more information.

Lines 235-246. Smith reverts to one of Davis's earliest scene lies with information about Ted Sherman. This furthers the characterization of both characters, as well as setting up more aura of danger around the mission.

Lines 247-250. Davis, in a final brief bit of conflict, insists Smith's report is not true, implying that any danger in this mission could not be so great.

Line 251. In the briefest of internalizations, Smith calls Davis a liar — showing the reader that *yes*, Smith got his information, *but* he is now moving into an adventure which could result in his death. In other words, the brief internalization serves to help the reader realize that Smith has indeed had a scene disaster.

LINKING YOUR SCENES: THE STRUCTURE OF SEQUEL

This appendix contains two excerpts. Commentary follows them.

EXCERPT 1

Excerpt is from chapter 13 of *Rage of Angels*, by Sidney Sheldon. William Morrow & Co., © 1980 by Sidney Sheldon.

1   Later, when Jennifer thought about that luncheon, she tried
2 to remember what they had talked about, what they had eaten,
3 who had stopped by the table to say hello to Adam, but all she
4 could remember was the nearness of Adam, his touch, his looks.
5 It was as though he had her in some kind of spell and she was
6 mesmerized, helpless to break it.
7   At one point Jennifer thought, *I know what to do, I'll make love*
8 *with him. Once. It can't be as wonderful as my fantasies. Then I'll be able*
9 *to get over him.*

Commentary

Although this sequel is very short, the progress from emotion to decision can be seen in its few words. Not classic in pattern, it nevertheless has the thrust of sequel.

Line 1. Establishes that this is a remembrance after the fact, which indicates that it is probably some form of sequel.

Lines 2-6. Although a direct statement of emotion is not found, clearly this is not a description of normal cognitive process; she *tried* to recall rationally, but could not. The implication is of confusion caused by her intense emotional reaction to Adam.

Lines 7-9. Sheldon, always likely to fragment structure for the sake of forward speed, skips over any logical analysis Jennifer may have gone through to get to a decision, and gives the decision straight away.

Note also that in this case the intensity of Jennifer's attraction to Adam is emphasized by the fact that the reader is shown no analytical thought process, or delay to think about the decision. (To put this another way, Sheldon's departure from classic sequel structure is for good reason: to better illustrate the intense, impetuous nature of the decision—which in turn emphasizes the intensity of the physical attraction.)

EXCERPT 2

Excerpt is from an as-yet-unpublished novel, by the author, © 1991, Jack M. Bickham.

1   The fall was quick and sickening. Johnnie's hands and arms
2 bashed against rock and support timbers as she flailed to catch
3 onto something, but before she could cushion her fall in any way,
4 she hit the bottom. Instead of the stunning solid impact she tried
5 to brace for, she hit with a shock into the coldest, blackest water
6 she had ever imagined.
7   The icy impact made her gasp, choking in some of the brack-
8 ish fluid. She was under—upside down and about to drown. Des-
9 peration took over. She flailed upward and got her head into the
10 air again, gagging and coughing. The bright blip of her flashlight
11 bobbed in the water beside her, throwing crazy patterns of bright-
12 ness on a bare rock ledge. She grabbed the flashlight and lunged
13 for the edge, catching it with one hand. Her breath whistled in
14 her lungs as she shook herself, trying to see more clearly.
15   Beginning to get control of her breathing spasms, she tossed
16 the flashlight up on the pool shelf, then got both elbows up over
17 the rocks and heaved herself convulsively up and out.
18   Bits of dirt and rock tumbled down, peppering her with the
19 aftermath of her plunge. Amazingly, she didn't seem to have any
20 broken bones. A violent spasm bent her double, and she retched
21 up some of the oily water she had swallowed. She couldn't seem
22 to stop shaking. She sprayed the flashlight beam around, first
23 looking up—the way she had fallen.
24   It looked like a long way up there, more than the twenty feet
25 she remembered from the charts. The walls were mostly rock,
26 chiseled out very smoothly, with only a half dozen vertical timbers
27 still in place from whatever bracing the miners had built when
28 they dug to this lower level so long ago. At the top, she could see
29 the shattered ends of the timbers that had given way under her
30 weight.
31   There was no way she could climb back up: no handholds,
32 no niches she could dig her toes into, and it was too wide to try
33 any kind of body-wedge tactic like the rock-climbers did on the
34 sheer face of Red Mountain. She was stuck down here. She had

35 been stupid!
36　　She mentally shook herself. No matter how dumb she had
37 been to forget to watch her step, it was done and she was in this
38 mess and what now?
39　　Her arms and legs had taken a beating, hitting against rock
40 and wood as she fell. Her head still had a ringing sound in it.
41 Using the flashlight to examine herself, she saw numerous bright
42 cuts and scratches, but nothing that seemed too serious.
43　　She hugged herself, but couldn't stop the shivering. It was
44 much colder at this lower level. Panic pounded on the door of her
45 mind, wanting to take over.
46　　Just try to be calm and rational, she told herself, and think.
47　　All right:
48　　She couldn't climb out from here. She was stuck, but good.
49 Should she look for another escape route, or sit tight in hopes
50 someone would find her before dehydration or exposure took her
51 out permanently?
52　　No one knew where she was—which was her own fault. But
53 wouldn't they start looking for her in another hour or two, and
54 spot her Jeep from the road?
55　　With a new sinking sensation, she knew the answer to that.
56 She had parked beyond the maintenance sheds to let the sun shine
57 through the windshield and keep the vehicle warm while she was
58 away from it. But when it was parked behind the sheds, it was
59 invisible from the road above.
60　　Panic knocked again. Remembering what she had discovered
61 on the upper level, she shuddered. *I have got to get out of here and*
62 *report this.*
63　　How was she going to do that?
64　　She couldn't climb out. How, then?
65　　Fighting to stay calm, she thought back to the old charts.
66 There had been some ventilation shafts marked on them. Could
67 a person climb out through one of them?
68　　This level extended more than a mile in both directions, she
69 remembered. It was intersected here and there by natural fis-
70 sures, cracks and caverns. She remembered someone saying that
71 some of those natural faultlines reached the surface, too.
72　　So what was she to do? Bumble back into the bowels of the
73 mountain, hoping for a lucky break?
74　　It wasn't quite that bad, she told herself. This was Level 2.
75 She knew there was a Level 3, and at that point she remembered
76 the chart showing another vertical shaft. She also remembered
77 that Level 3 had been started only a few hundred yards to the
78 south.
79　　Which way was south? She shone the flashlight left and right,
80 into the tunnels extending in both directions off the seepage pool
81 into which she had plunged. To her left, the flashlight beam
82 stopped less than twenty feet away, shining on rubble that filled

83 | the tunnel in that direction. Swinging her beam to the other end
84 | of the shaft, she saw an uneven carpet of fallen rock splinters and
85 | some support timbers leaning at spooky angles. But the tunnel
86 | in that direction appeared to be intact.
87 | So she didn't have to strain her brain trying to figure out
88 | which way to go, she thought with dismay. There was only one
89 | direction open to her.
90 | The little-girl part of her started to yammer and bawl. *I don't*
91 | *wanna go, I'm too scared!*
92 | She gasped for air, fighting to regain control of her feelings.
93 | How long could she last down here in this cold darkness? Long
94 | enough to be found alive? Could she sit tight and *count on that?*
95 | She thought of Luke—momentarily yearned for him. But then
96 | her mind conjured another image: Butt Peabody. Would Luke
97 | know what to do? She doubted it. Would Butt? Yes. Somehow
98 | Butt would know.
99 | But Butt wasn't here. If she was going to get out of this mess
100 | any time soon, she had to do it on her own. And something told
101 | her she couldn't just sit and wait.
102 | Getting shakily to her feet, she eased her way around the
103 | black seepage pool that had cushioned her fall and scared her
104 | halfwitted at the same time. Beyond it, her flashlight lit up the
105 | first few yards of blackness that filled the only mineshaft open to
106 | her. She limped into it.

Commentary

In a chapter some pages earlier in this story, the character Johnnie Baker had sought to discover whether someone had broken into an old mine shaft. The scene question—*"Will Johnnie discover signs of a break-in?"*—was answered *"Yes, but!"* as she discovered a hidden body, but then fell through booby-trapped planks covering a vertical shaft into which she plunged. This scene-ending disaster also ended a chapter, after which there was a change of viewpoint to other characters in other trouble of their own.

This segment marks the return of viewpoint to Johnnie; no story time has elapsed since she fell through the broken planks.

Lines 1-14. Continue the action of the disaster to make sure the reader remembers exactly where Johnnie was left at the earlier chapter-ending.

Line 15. Johnnie begins to react. Her sequel opens. The fact that she can't seem to stop shaking (Lines 21-22) shows *emotional* as well as physical shock.

Lines 21-30. These lines provide reader orientation to Johnnie's plight as Johnnie herself experiences the knowledge.

Lines 31-32. The thought portion of the sequel begins. Johnnie begins to analyze her data.

Lines 34-35. The statement about being stupid shows her reverting a moment to emotion—anger with herself. Emotion often tends to return like this in sequels after the character has begun to try to think. Here, you may wish to note that Johnnie is *characterized* by the nature of her emotion: She does not experience terror like many would; her emotion is tougher—irritation with herself.

Lines 44-45. Again emotion tries to take over, but Johnnie is tough.

Line 46. Here she lectures herself, in effect, to "get on with the thinking part of this sequel!"

Lines 48-50. In classic patterns, she begins reviewing her situation, and analyzing it.

Lines 60-61. Panic—emotion—tries to return, but again she beats it back.

Lines 61-62. She moves to a new general decision—to get out—and immediately goes on to trying to come up with a plan to achieve this broad goal.

Lines 64-89. All aspects of her plight—and possible new goal-oriented actions—are analyzed.

Lines 90-91. Still again, fear tries to paralyze her.

Line 92. Lines such as this—showing the character's continuing awareness of strong emotion—but determination not to wallow helplessly—add realism to portrayal of the total response to a disaster; in real life, we seldom move quickly from emotion to pure logic; feelings keep recurring; thus we show such a pattern here.

Lines 93-101. Johnnie considers and rejects the most likely motives she could have for sitting tight—when sitting tight is the last thing the author wants her to do.

Lines 102-106. Having worked through her emotion, thought and decision-making processes, she starts toward her new goal with *action*—limping into the mineshaft in search of a way out.

VARIATIONS IN THE INTERNAL STRUCTURE OF SCENE AND SEQUEL

This appendix contains one excerpt. Commentary follows.

Excerpt is from chapter 8 of *Tiebreaker*, by Jack M. Bickham. Tor Books, © 1989 by Jack M. Bickham. This sequel resumes reader contact with the character Partek after plot changes to several other viewpoints. When last seen, he was fleeing the town of Browning, Montana, after a narrow escape from capture.

1	*Swift Current, Saskatchewan*
2	The prairie of Saskatchewan looked like it extended a thou-
3	sand miles.
4	In some directions it did.
5	Standing in front of his motel unit, Dominic Partek looked
6	out over the low sprawl of the town of Swift Current, and watched
7	faint cloud-shadows drift across the face of the naked grass hil-
8	locks. It was afternoon, hot.
9	Partek had to decide where next he would flee.
10	He delayed the decision by staring at the prairie, letting the
11	sadness move through him.
12	The sadness was unrelated to the danger that choked him.
13	He searched for a reason for it and found one: this barren country
14	reminded him of the flatlands of Serbia around Surcin and Beo-
15	grad.
16	He had imagined that nostalgia for his homeland was long-
17	since behind him. But in his current predicament the landscape
18	had brought it back.
19	Partek lit one Players off another and turned his gaze to the
20	bug-encrusted front of his truck. He had driven hard and slept a
21	long time. Now he had to decide his next step.
22	He faced the cruelest kind of dilemma. If he went back, the
23	punishment would be severe, possibly death. But if he reverted
24	to his agonizing decision to defect to the West, he might be found
25	and killed anyway; and certainly his family—so long thought

26 | lost— would pay.
27 | *Whatever I do,* he thought, *there will be suffering.*
28 | He was sick of it—sick of suffering, of dilemmas, of uncer-
29 | tainty and loss . . . sick of himself.
30 | He remembered his childhood in Surcin. His father had al-
31 | ways been ill, had sometimes been drunk and violent. In those
32 | times he had beaten Dominic with a cold, terrifying fury. The boy
33 | had grown up with terror. Usually his mother had been able to
34 | intervene before the beating went too far. Sometimes Alexi Partek
35 | beat her, too, for intervening.
36 | Dominic's mother, gaunt and haggard, had always held a full-
37 | time job at a bearing factory. But she had always loved him, had
38 | held him and smiled at him when he did well, protected him as
39 | best she could. And sometimes in the evenings when his father
40 | was gone she had sung the old songs. Dominic had adored her,
41 | would have done anything for her.
42 | So in school he worked very hard, and was a fine student.
43 | His father sneered at his accomplishments, saying they would not
44 | improve his chances in life.
45 | Dominic was good in athletics, too, which his mother told
46 | him should be no surprise: his father, long ago, before his tragic
47 | injuries at Stalingrad, had been athletic too. His father, Dominic
48 | was told, had been a great hero at Stalingrad, and this was why
49 | he limped so, experienced such constant pain, was sometimes vio-
50 | lently ill, did not have adequate lungs.
51 | Alexi Partek was from the Ukraine, she told Dominic, and
52 | should have been compensated by the Russians for his heroism
53 | in the war against Hitler. That the Russians had discarded and
54 | ignored him after his great service was only another proof that
55 | the Russians were evil men.
56 | Dominic's father had only one serious conversation with him
57 | during his growing-up. On that occasion, Alexi Partek told his
58 | son that he should not believe his mother's railings against the
59 | Soviet Union. It had been an honor to give up his health for the
60 | USSR, Alexi told his son, and if there was a reason now why he
61 | drank sometimes, and fell into fits of the blackest and most violent
62 | melancholy, it was because circumstances forced him to live here
63 | in Yugoslavia, Martina Partek's homeland, rather than in his be-
64 | loved Ukraine. His wife, Alexi Partek said bitterly, understood
65 | nothing. She was *govno.* Everything about Yugoslavia was *govno.*
66 | Disagreements of this sort were part of the fabric of Dominic's
67 | childhood. He worked hard to please his mother and to avoid his
68 | father's fists. He led his class through school.
69 | In 1966, Dominic had graduated from high school and en-
70 | tered the Yugoslav army by conscription. It should have been a
71 | happy development with hope for the future, but at almost the
72 | same time something wonderful and something disastrous hap-
73 | pened in the family. His mother, astonishingly, told him that she

74 | was pregnant. And his father, after a ghastly scene, ran away.
75 | Sending her son off to the army, Martina Partek was pale but
76 | resolute.
77 | "I will manage," she told him.
78 | "Father will come back," Dominic told her.
79 | "No." She was like ice-covered stone. He could sense her
80 | inner-trembling, but God, she was strong. He had always known
81 | she was strong, but in this moment her strength awed him. "He
82 | will not come back. But if he tried, he can never stay here again."
83 | "Mother!"
84 | "You are a man now," she told him with an eerie calm. "I will
85 | tell you this. Alexi has gone away because of this child in my belly.
86 | You heard the shouting, the threats and insults. We cannot feed
87 | another child, he says. We are too old, he says. But I tell you this,
88 | my son: one time, long ago, there was another child in my belly;
89 | Alexi shouted and raved, and I . . . had an end put to that preg-
90 | nancy. Still sometimes at night, in my chair, I look up from my
91 | sewing, and there at the dark-night window I see the face of that
92 | child of mine I did not allow to be born. I will not lose this child.
93 | I will have this child and raise this child. I will do that. Alexi is
94 | gone because he could not confront another child. He will not
95 | come back to me because I have chosen this child over him."
96 | Martina Partek's eyes looked far away, and her jaw set. "I do
97 | not think I will see Alexi's face at the window in the dark of night."
98 | It had been a grim home-leaving, but once in the army train-
99 | ing camp Dominic had put it behind him as best he could, and
100 | did what he always had done: fight to excel. Almost all of his
101 | pitiful monthly check was mailed back to Surcin. Months passed
102 | and he finished basic training and was selected for special code
103 | and cipher school near Sarajevo.
104 | While he was in that school, word came that his father had
105 | died in Moscow. Dominic was granted five days' leave to attend to
106 | final arrangements. By the time he arrived in Moscow, he learned
107 | that his father's body had already been cremated, and the "estate"
108 | amounted to a cheap watch, a handful of unidentified pills, a few
109 | items of clothing, and unpaid rent in a cheap rooming house.
110 | Under "Identity" on the certificate of death, the inspectors had
111 | written *Veteran. Unemployed.*
112 | His leave time running out, Dominic returned to his new
113 | post. He wrote a long letter to his mother in Surcin, and enclosed
114 | a small extra amount of money, borrowed from another trainee.
115 | Two weeks later, this envelope was returned to him with the
116 | stamp on it: *UNKNOWN.*
117 | Dominic remailed the letter, telling himself the return had
118 | been a bureaucratic mistake. It came back again. Badly alarmed,
119 | he sought emergency leave. He was told he had just had an emer-
120 | gency leave.
121 | For three more weeks he stewed and waited for the leave that

122 would come automatically at the conclusion of the first phase of
123 his intelligence training. He considered going to Surcin without
124 official leave, but such disobedience of orders would have been
125 contrary to every fiber of his morality. So he waited, scared.

126   When he finally got to Surcin, he went at once to the tiny
127 wood shack where he had grown up. He found another family
128 there. Their name was Rishtek. They knew nothing about his
129 mother. He talked to neighbors. They said Martina Partek had
130 simply vanished, evidently taking her few possessions with her.

131   Frantic now, Dominic called on the militia. But they pointed
132 out that his mother had taken her things with her, so foul play
133 seemed highly unlikely. They agreed at last to file a report. Domi-
134 nic, although young, was experienced enough to know what hap-
135 pened to reports when they were tossed into the maw of the bu-
136 reaucracy.

137   His leave ran out. He used every moment available to search,
138 but he didn't know where to search, or how. He spent his last day
139 of leave walking up and down streets in Belgrade, thinking that
140 somehow he would just look up, and by magic there she would
141 be. He realized that he might as well be looking in some other
142 city; he had chosen Belgrade for his blind wanderings only be-
143 cause it was nearest Surcin.

144   All through 1966, as he finished one school and was immedi-
145 ately sent to another, a haunted Dominic Partek wrote letters,
146 filled out enquiry forms, bombarded the mail with questions. He
147 was convinced that his mother would not have deserted him if
148 she had been in control; he was sure something dreadful had
149 happened to her.

150   What had happened to her? And to the child she had been
151 carrying?

152   His letters and tracer forms came back stamped or scribbled
153 on with the stupid monosyllables of drones and functionaries:
154 *NOTED. NAME ON FILE. NO RECORD. FORWARDED. RE-*
155 *TURNED. NO ACTION. UNKNOWN. HELD PEND FORM 860.*
156 *NO DOCUMENTS.* Twice he got short leaves and rushed to Surcin
157 or Belgrade again, but no one knew anything. Old friends shook
158 their heads sadly and turned away. These things happened.

159   By the summer of 1968, Dominic's hopes had gone. He com-
160 pleted the last phase of intelligence school and was assigned as an
161 attache in the Yugoslav embassy in Moscow. There he met a man
162 named Kudirka, a Lithuanian who worked in the Soviet govern-
163 ment. Their friendship became close, and on a brisk October eve-
164 ning, walking near the walls of the Kremlin, Kudirka bluntly
165 asked Dominic if he had ever considered a career "with a major
166 organization in the field."

167   "You must know I am attached to the UDBA," Dominic told
168 him.

169   "I have in mind our own organization," Kudirka replied.

170   "You mean the KGB?"

171   His friend smiled.

172   "You are a member of the KGB?" Dominic pressed, aston-
173   ished.

174   "Please do not misunderstand me," Kudirka said. "I do not
175   suggest that you should represent my organization against your
176   own. Your loyalty is unquestioned and of great interest to us. No.
177   What I suggest is an arrangement under which your files could
178   be transferred to our offices on a permanent basis. You would
179   become one of us. We have a great need for men of your loyalty,
180   intelligence and integrity. We would provide additional training.
181   Within two years' time, you would in all likelihood be an attache
182   like myself at a Soviet embassy in another part of the world."

183   "But my government would never agree to such an arrange-
184   ment!"

185   "It is not impossible," Kudirka told him.

186   "My tour of duty extends another two and one-half years."

187   "It is not a major impediment."

188   Then Kudirka told Partek what he would be paid, and how
189   he would be trained. He spoke of advancement, world opportuni-
190   ties.

191   They were magic words. Partek had already begun to see the
192   parochialism of the UDBA, and its limited role in the world. He
193   was a good communist, and despite his suspicion of things Rus-
194   sian, considered the KGB a valiant and praiseworthy operation—
195   the best on the planet.

196   And here was his chance to become part of it. He had no
197   family to hold him back.

198   The decision was made. With amazing alacrity, the Yugoslav
199   bureaucracy spat out the reams of necessary paperwork. Before
200   Christmas, Partek reported to an officer in the great old stone
201   headquarters building on Moscow's Dzerzhinsky Square.

202   *How far I have come!* he thought in mute wonderment. Then,
203   thinking of his lost mother and the baby, he added, *And how far*
204   *will I go, in honor of your memory!*

205   His real life's work began on that day. . . .

206   So long ago, Partek thought now, still standing on the breezy,
207   sunny pavement of his motel in Canada. He was filled with sad-
208   ness. He wondered what he would have done on that day so long
209   ago if he could have foreseen what he knew now, if he could have
210   guessed the disillusionment and treachery.

211   He had thought he was being clever enough in the way he
212   cautiously contacted one of his counterparts in the CIA. He only
213   needed to know at that point how a transfer of loyalties might be
214   handled, how he might turn himself over, be hidden, get an even-
215   tual new identity and occupation so he could live out his life in
216   the West.

217   At that time he had not even been sure he could take such a

218 horrendous step, despite the years of disillusionment with his So-
219 viet masters. He was, in contacting the CIA acquaintance, only
220 gathering information for a contingency.
221   And he was so careful . . . so circumspect.
222   But not careful enough. The American FBI knew of it almost
223 at once, and made a contact with him. That was not so bad, but
224 somehow his KGB masters also got wind of his change of perspec-
225 tive . . . possibly a difference in his disposition at work, possibly
226 something of more substance — not enough to justify stern action
227 on their part, but a subtle warning.
228   That was when they had allowed him to learn about his fam-
229 ily, after all these years. So he would know what he had to lose if
230 his loyalty ever faltered.
231   They must have thought they were being very clever, letting
232 him uncover the old archival information "by mistake." But in
233 reality their ploy had backfired. Rather than frightening Partek,
234 the ruse had disillusioned and enraged him. *They knew this for*
235 *years, and never told me. And it was my right to know!* His shock was
236 profound.
237   His American contacts pressed him for a final decision.
238   He agonized and delayed.
239   *"They suspect you, Dominic. Better to come over now."*
240   *"I cannot defect now! They will retaliate in Belgrade!"*
241   *"What if we could fix that?"*
242   *"Fix? Fix what? How? You cannot control the Soviets!"*
243   *"What if we could get her out, so there could never be any reprisals?"*
244   *"You could do that?"*
245   *"We can try. . . ."*
246   So Partek had fled, buying time. But that had been a mistake,
247 because now, by his actions, he stood convicted by his KGB mas-
248 ters. He knew they were looking for him. To make matters worse,
249 both the CIA and FBI were also chasing him "for his own protec-
250 tion."
251   So that now all he could do was keep hiding . . . see if the
252 CIA's promises were fulfilled. If they were, there was hope. If the
253 CIA failed him, he was doomed, like his family.
254   A truck horn sounded on the highway beyond the motel en-
255 trance. The sound jarred Partek out of his reverie, reminding him
256 of the danger and the need to move. He closed his motel unit
257 door, tossed his cigarette into a puddle on the pavement, and
258 climbed into his truck.
259   He had to keep moving — do the unexpected.
260   It was the only thing he was sure about right now.

Commentary

This is a very complex sequel which not only has to reestablish the character's whereabouts and planned next moves after a disaster several chapters

earlier, but for the first time must explain to the reader at least two portions of the character's earlier life: his youth and recruitment into the KGB, and his much-later disillusionment and temptation to defect to the West. Thus the sequel must contain variations from classic sequel pattern.

Lines 2-3. Reestablishes the place where action resumes.

Lines 5-6. Establishes Partek's viewpoint.

Line 9. Shows that Partek has entered the thought segment of his sequel, and establishes his intention to find a new goal.

Lines 10-11. Establishes Partek's emotional state.

Line 12. Makes it clear that Partek's sadness is not in response to his last disaster, but to some earlier ones.

Lines 13-15. Stimulus and response: The land reminds him of his former homeland . . . thus setting off the memories which follow. *He does not remember without having a physical, outside reason.*

Lines 19-21. Fill-in action that took place "between chapters" involving this character.

Lines 21-27. Repeat his need for a decision in this sequel, and show that he truly faces a dilemma.

Lines 28-29. Here Partek's present emotional state is given. These two lines could just as well as started the entire sequel.

Line 30. Begins the lengthy segment in which Partek's background, previously hidden from the reader, is brought out in detail. The segment starts with narration.

Lines 75-76. Begins a portion of a scene imbedded in the sequel.

Lines 95-97. The scene fragment ends and we return to narration.

Lines 167-168. Another part of a scene begins to play inside the sequel structure, which has continued to be narration of Partek's past as he recalls in the review segment of the thought portion of his sequel.

Lines 188-191. This scene fragment ends and narration resumes.

Line 202. Begins a brief flashback to a sequel Partek had long ago.

Lines 206-207. Returns to the present, Partek still standing on the pavement, *no present story time having elapsed.*

Lines 211-212. Begins a segment of the sequel in which Partek still reviews past history—but of much more recent vintage. This segment serves to tell the reader a lot about how Partek got into his present predicament.

Line 237. A quick description of one or more sequels long ago.

Lines 239-245. The fragment of another scene, this from the more recent past and italicized for added emphasis.

Line 251. Back to the present, and the sequel decision.

Line 259. A refining of the sequel decision, clearly showing what he will do next.

Thus the varied pattern of this sequel has been:

Sequel:

Present time, establishment of place.

Thought segment begins.

Narrative move back to character history.

Scene fragment in sequel. (With Mother)

Resumption of memory narrative.
Scene fragment in sequel. (With recruiter)
Resumption of memory narrative.
Return to present sequel time.
Narrative move back to more recent memory.
Scene fragment in sequel. (With CIA)
Resumption of memory narrative.
Return to present sequel time.
New decision and immediate new goal.

SPECIALIZED SCENE TECHNIQUES

This appendix contains one excerpt. Commentary follows.

Excerpt is from chapter 5 of *Katie, Kelly and Heck*, by Jack M. Bickham. Doubleday & Co., © 1973 by Jack M. Bickham.

This excerpt is from a comic novel in which Katherine (Katie) Blanscombe goes to a remote frontier town in the old West to claim her half of an unspecified inheritance from a long-lost uncle. Upon arrival, Katie and her young ward, Heck, meet Mike Kelly, who was the dead uncle's business partner and co-inherited with Katie. Katie is attracted to Mike, but denies it to herself, and quickly takes a dislike to him. The following action takes place on the evening following her noon arrival on the stagecoach; she has just answered a knock on the door of the hotel room she shares with young Heck; it is the desk clerk.

1	"Beggin' your pardon, ma'am, but you have a caller in the
2	lobby."
3	"A caller?"
4	"Mister Ray Root, ma'am. He said to say, if you don't know
5	who he is, he runs a cafe and casino that's in competition with
6	Mike Kelly."
7	Katie hesitated. She had no idea what the man might want.
8	But if he was in competition with Mike Kelly, she thought, he
9	might not particularly *like* Mike Kelly, and that gave them some-
10	thing in common. Besides, she was curious.
11	"Tell Mister Root," she said, "that I'll be there directly."
12	. . . .
13	In the small front room that served as a lobby, only one per-
14	son was in evidence: a tall, dark-coated man with rather long black
15	hair that glistened under a heavy layer of oil. He wore a flowered
16	vest and wide mustaches, thin-legged pants and slightly muddied
17	black boots that shone, nevertheless, like patent leather. His flat-
18	brimmed hat, beaded, was in his hands.
19	"Miss Blanscombe?" he said, showing a great number of

20 small, even white teeth.

21 "Yes," Katie said, extending her hand.

22 "Enchanted," the man said, clicking his heels and bending
23 from the waist to kiss her fingers. "Allow me to present myself. I
24 am Ray Root."

25 The finger-kissing was shock enough; Katie had never ex-
26 pected continental manners in Salvation when she had only read
27 about them in a civilized place like Cleveland. But Ray Root's
28 entire appearance and manner quietly bowled her over. He was
29 tall and slender, and given to a flinty kind of handsomeness that
30 was modified slightly by wrinkles which, on close inspection, hin-
31 ted he was either older than he first appeared, or more dissipated.
32 He smelled of tobacco and clove and coffee, and although his
33 smile was friendly, there was something behind his quick dark
34 eyes that made Katie's pores shrink as if his eyes were undressing
35 her. Katie made some tentative decisions about him: (a) he was
36 attractive, (b) he was aware of it, and (c) he was a cad. In her mood,
37 this did not necessarily make her dislike him.

38 "How do you do, Mister Root?" she asked formally.

39 "Three things," Root said, continuing to smile brightly.
40 "First, allow me to add my small welcome to an attractive new-
41 comer to our fair city. You'll find, Miss Blanscombe, that first im-
42 pressions indicate a raw, frontier hamlet; but Salvation has much
43 beneath the surface, including a small but active cultural life."

44 "Indeed?" Katie said, surprised again.

45 "Indeed," Root said. "Second, may I say that I have heard
46 about the lawsuit you have brought against certain, ah, establish-
47 ments, and if I may offer my support, please don't hesitate to
48 ask."

49 "In view of the fact that you said you compete with Mike
50 Kelly," Katie said, "I can understand your interest."

51 Ray Root frowned and his mustaches twitched. "Yes, yes. But
52 actually, Miss Blanscombe, my interest is not in eliminating com-
53 petition. Far from it! I believe competition is at the heart of Amer-
54 ica's progress, the kernel of her way of life, if you will. But I must
55 say that I share your concern for establishments which fall under
56 suspicion of operating, ah, shall we say . . . less than in a manner
57 that is aboveboard."

58 "I assume, Mister Root, you'll get to the point."

59 "Call me Ray," Root urged. "I hope to be your friend."

60 "The point, Mister Root."

61 "The point. Yes, of course. The point is simplicity itself. I
62 offer support. I have no ax to grind. If I can help, you have but
63 to ask."

64 "And the third point?" Katie probed.

65 Ray Root blinked. "The third point?"

66 Katie was amused. She had the feeling he was harmless
67 enough. "You mentioned three points you wanted to make."

68   "Oh, yes. The third point, Miss Blanscombe — may I call you
69   Katherine? The third point, Katherine, is that I wish to offer to
70   make myself available to you tomorrow, at your convenience. I
71   feel sure that a comprehensive tour of Salvation and its environs
72   would interest you, and enhance your understanding of the gen-
73   eral situation. I understand you have a young brother, and he,
74   too, of course, is invited."
75   Katie hid her frown. He was going a little too fast for her.
76   Her natural caution asserted itself. "I appreciate the kind offer,
77   Mister Root. However . . ."
78   The front door slammed open and rain gushed in. Katie
79   turned, startled, and saw Mike Kelly, hatless and muddy to the
80   knees, charge into the lobby. He caught her with a fiercely angry
81   glance, swung toward her and pointed a shaking finger at her.
82   "There you are!" he bellowed. "By God, the two of you are
83   in cahoots already!"
84   Ray Root blanched slightly. "See here, Mike —"
85   "Shut up, Ray!" Mike stormed, stalking toward them.
86   Katie stiffened as her own anger rose magically. "*What*, may
87   I ask, is the meaning of this? What are you doing here, Mister
88   Kelly, and —"
89   Mike Kelly towered over her. His face was red and his eyes
90   bulged as if they might explode. "I just heard about that silly
91   blankety lawsuit, *that's* what it's all about! What the hell kind of
92   person are you, anyway? What are you trying to do? If you think
93   you'll get to first base with some stupid maneuver like that,
94   you've —"
95   "*Mister* Kelly," Katie cut in sharply. "I'll thank you, sir, to take
96   your bad manners elsewhere, or my attorney will have another
97   charge to file against you, that of battery."
98   "*Battery!*" Mike bellowed. "I'll battery you! I'll charge your —
99   I'll —"
100   Katie turned icily to Ray Root. "You were saying — Ray?"
101   Root smiled uncertainly. "I was saying that a tour —"
102   "What are you pulling here?" Mike Kelly cut in just as loudly
103 as before. "Listen, woman! You get to town at noon, and the same
104 day you file some stupid idiot lawsuit against me and then start
105 getting thick as hops with the worst gambler and drink-watering —"
106   Ray Root said huskily, "Don't go too far, Mike."
107   Mike Kelly ignored the threat in his voice. Mike was past
108 worrying about threats. "I'm talking to her, Ray. You keep your
109 face shut, see?"
110   "But I am not talking to *you*," Katie told Mike. "My attorney
111 has said all I wish to say to you, sir."
112   "What do you want to *do* this to me for?" Mike cried. "I run
113 a nice place and I never had a cross word with Hank in my entire
114 life! I loved the guy! And then you come in here and start plotting
115 with *this* no'count card sharper —"

116   "That," Katie clipped, "will be enough."
117   Mike stared at her in disbelief. "I came here to talk."
118   "You came here to bluster and threaten. It won't work. I have
119 nothing more to say to you."
120   "You won't even *listen* to me?" Mike Kelly asked, and he hon-
121 estly looked like he could have wept in frustration.
122   "You've turned an honest business into a den of thieves,"
123 Katie told him.
124   "I —!"
125   She turned to Ray Root. "I don't know what my schedule will
126 be tomorrow — Ray. But possibly a tour of the area with you would
127 be not only informative, but very pleasant. Could you call about
128 noon?"
129   Ray Root's grin was oily enough to fuel a tanker. "Be my
130 pleasure, little lady."
131   "You're going out with *him*?" Mike Kelly gasped, stunned.
132   "Is it any of your business?" Katie shot back imperiously.
133   "You're crazy!" Mike groaned. "I come over here to talk *sense*,
134 and you —"
135   "Good night, Ray," Katie said warmly to Ray Root. "And
136 thank you."
137   Root grinned and shook her hand this time. He looked aw-
138 fully pleased.
139   Mike Kelly, however, looked like someone who had just been
140 run down by a freight train. His face drained of color.
141   In a voice that was almost inaudible he whispered, "I came
142 to *talk*."
143   Katie turned her back on him and marched toward her room.
144   She was delighted. So he thought he was a ladies' man, did
145 he, with his hotel full of nasty girls and his lovely wavy hair and
146 beautiful blue eyes! Well, she had showed *him* a thing or two — and
147 she wasn't finished yet by a long shot!

Commentary

My problem long ago as the author of this segment of the novel remains
fresh in my mind: Ray Root is obviously a "cad," as Katie so archaically
puts it, and even in his comic exaggeration here it's pretty obvious to the
reader that he's not a man to be trusted, and is up to no good. Why, then,
would Katie ever agree to go out with him? (And I *needed* this to happen
in my plot!) Analysis of the excerpt shows how I managed it.

Lines 4-6. Introduce the other character who will be in the scene to
come. Again here, on a smaller scale, why would a young woman in a
strange, scary frontier town go downstairs to talk with a perfect stranger?
The answer: Provide her with a specific stimulus, the words "in competition with Mike Kelly."

Lines 7-10. Katie's internalization to that stimulus, ending in a decision to go do what she otherwise would not have done.

Lines 13-24. Exaggerated comic description of Root. But the comic description *can be — and is — also used as stimulus.*

Lines 25-37. Katie's internalization to Root's appearance and manners. But in her angry mood, she will talk to him.

Line 38. Her response.

Line 39. Root launches into his game plan with the first of his "three things."

Line 44. Stimulus.

Line 45. Repetition of the word to start Root's response.

Line 58. Katie starts a comic stimulus and response with Root over "the point" — "the third point."

Line 65. Root looks stupid. This is a stimulus.

Lines 66-67. Katie's internalization-conclusion about Root, natural enough, but as the reader knows from other earlier parts of the novel, *dead wrong.*

Line 67. Katie sends a new repetitive stimulus.

Line 68. Root again repeats wordage and launches his real scene goal, to get her to go out with him.

Lines 75-77. Katie's internalization. She is about to say no. She would *never* go out with this stranger under ordinary circumstances. (How can the author make her do it?)

Line 78. New stimulus. *Scene interruptus.* Mike Kelly arrives to interrupt the Katie-Root scene with a Mike-Katie scene.

Line 84. Root tries to make the scene a threesome. This as we know can be confusing.

Line 85. So Mike Kelly shuts him up, effectively making most of what follows the desired one-on-one conflict.

Lines 89-94. Mike in effect tells about one or more scenes that he has had in the hidden story recently.

Lines 95-99. Their conflict sharpens.

Line 100. Katie calls Root by his first name for the first time, obviously to get back at Mike and further infuriate him. This sets the pattern for her decision to follow.

Line 106. Root tries to make it a three-way again.

Lines 107-109. Mike effectively makes it a one-on-one again.

Lines 112-115. Mike further reveals what he really wants to know — why he wants to talk. He simply can't understand her. (And incidentally everything he says here is the gospel truth, *and the reader knows it.*)

Lines 130-132. Katie has been completely turned around from her internalization-decision in lines 75-77. Mike's interruption of her scene with Root has given her sufficient cause for the author-desired effect — to have her throw caution to the winds and go out with the buzzard.

Line 131. We see Mike's emotion as disaster falls on him.

Lines 137-138. Root looks pleased. He knows things have turned out wonderfully for him in this scene.

Lines 141-142. Poor Mike repeats one more time his thwarted scene goal.

Lines 144-147. Katie starts her sequel in classic form. *Emotion*: delighted. *Thought*: given in these lines. *Decision*: not clear yet, but obviously she has more plans.

The pattern for the entire segment, structurally:

Scene 1

Goal: Root's, to get Katie to go out.
Katie's, to learn what Root wants.
Scene question: *Will* he get her to go out?
Conflict: Root's deviousness opposed to Katie's probing.
Interrupted by:

Scene 2

Goal: Mike's. He wants to talk.
Scene question: *Will* he get her to talk?
Conflict: Katie won't talk.
Disaster: For Mike.
Answer to Mike's scene question: No. (End of Scene 2)

Resumption of Scene 1

Disaster: For Root, none. He's a bad guy so that's fine.
For Katie, yes, although she doesn't know it yet.
Mike's oral sequel to his scene.
Katie's thought sequel to hers.

Thus what we have here, in a seemingly simple and harmless little comic western plot, is a fairly complex juggling of stimuli and responses and parts of scenes to provide sufficient motivation for a character to decide finally to do something decidedly uncharacteristic of her.

It's in unusual circumstances such as this that understanding structure gives the writer extra tools in her arsenal.

INDEX

Conversational structure, 3
Crime fiction, 68

D

Dark Wind, The, 135
Deadly Shade of Gold, A, 108
Decision, 163; and multiple viewpoint, 101
Description, 156; comic, 162
Detective fiction, 68; viewpoint in, 88
Dialogue, 26, 47-48, 54-55, 112-113,
    135-136, 142; and stimulus and
    response, 15-16
Diary form, in fiction, 2-3
Dickens, Charles, 3, 7
Direction, errors in, 38
Disaster, 30, 31, 47, 48, 106, 107-108, 144,
    148, 163; and chapter ending, 117-
    118; concealment of, 75-76;
    contrived, 91; and emotional
    response, 102; to end scene, 26-28,
    59-60; ending short of, 75-76; errors
    in, 37-40; final, 129; and multiple
    viewpoint, 101; and narrative
    progress, 44-45; "no," 42; in novel,
    126; pacing, 64; reactions to, 51-52;
    and sequel, 51-52, 79-80; subplots
    and, 96; and suspense, 122; viewpoint
    change, 100, 101; viewpoint
    character, 11; "Yes, but," 59
Document novel, 3
Documentary structure, 3
Drama, and structure, 94-97
Dropshot, 133-134

E

Emotional response, 51, 53-55, 57, 61, 100,
    145, 148, 149, 162-163; coolness of,
    88-89; and disaster, 102; and pacing,
    67; in sequel, 80, 107
Ending, 7, 9, 10, 75-76; with disaster, 26-28,
    47; of scene, 47
Epistolary form, 2
Errors, most common, 83
Exercise, 30; disasters, 60-62; planning and
    working cards, 46; scenes and
    working cards, 82; sequels and
    working cards, 60-62; on structure,
    39; working cards and plotting, 39-40

External pressure, 82

F

Fictional "documentary," 3
Fictional journal or diary, 2-3
Fill-in action, 156
Finality, errors in, 38
First-person narrator, 3, 133
First-person novel, 3
Flashback, 78, 82, 110, 156
Forfeit, 8
Form, defined, 1
Forms, of novels, 3-4
Fragmented structure, 78, 145-146; and
    action, 76-77; prologue and, 123; and
    sequels, 77
Francis, Dick, 8

G

Goal, 10, 24-26, 30, 42, 106, 142, 163;
    conflict and, 66; and dominant
    viewpoint, 100; example, 10-11;
    immediacy of, 32-33; main character
    and, 124; of novel, 123-124; and
    opposition characters, 114-115;
    pacing and, 66-67; restatement of,
    126; short term, 25-26, 96, 124; and
    significance, 90; statement of, 75, 80;
    and viewpoint character, 4
Goals, and dominant viewpoint, 100
Great Expectations, 7

H

Hailey, Arthur, 70
Hero. *See* Protagonist
Hidden story, 98, 102, 106, 129
Higgins, Jack, 8, 132
Hillerman, Tony, 135
Hook, 134
Hotel, 70-71

I

Illogical disagreement, 90
Immediacy, 14-15, 16-17, 32-33, 59-60;
    errors in, 38
Internal conflict, 43
Internalization, 17-18, 21, 43, 77, 85, 87,
    136, 143, 144, 161; action scenes and,